Ann —

What a joy it is to work with you!

Merry Christmas

Ellen Long

JAMES MEANS
ARCHITECT

THE ARCHITECTURE *of* JAMES MEANS, GEORGIA CLASSICIST

by
William R. Mitchell, Jr.

photography by
James R. Lockhart

A Golden Coast Book
for
Southern Architecture Foundation, Inc.
2001

Southern Architecture Foundation, Inc.,
was created to promote understanding and appreciation of
Southern architecture and associated arts through:
Location, acquisition, organization, and conservation of related historic records and documents;
Identification, preservation, and restoration of historic structures, landscapes, and decorative arts and crafts;
Research, analysis, and synthesis of information related to the subject of the mission;
Publication of scholarly works resulting from these efforts;
Educational programs such as lectures and tours.

Southern Architecture Foundation, Inc.
1750 Peachtree Street, NW
Atlanta, Georgia 30309
Telephone: 404/733-6565

ILLUSTRATION CREDITS
All contemporary photographs, execpt as noted below, are by James R. Lockhart.
Atlanta History Center: 12 (bottom), 14 (top left), 15 (top right and center right), 19 (top), 20 (top and bottom left), 22, 23, 24, 25, 26, 31 (right), 32, 33 (bottom right), 42 (bottom), 47 (bottom), 49 (bottom), 51, 63 (bottom), 67 (bottom), 68, 73 (top), 81 (bottom), 83 (top), 84 (bottom), 85 (bottom), 89 (bottom), 93 (bottom), 98 (left), 110 (top), 125, 133 (right, top and bottom), 136 (bottom), 140, 149 (top), 153 (bottom), 155 (bottom), 164, 167 (top left), 169 (bottom);
Vivian Noble DuBose: 13 (top left);
Mrs. Gould B. (Laura Plowden) Hagler, Jr.: 9;
Family of Jesse Jones: 14 (right);
Mr. and Mrs. Jeremiah D. Luxemburger: 19 (bottom);
Van Jones Martin: 13 (bottom right), 14 (bottom left), 86, 87 (bottom), 88, 89 (top);
Mary Catherine Means: 12 (top), 13 (top right), 17, 20 (bottom right), 27 (top);
William R. Mitchell, Jr.: 14 (second from top on left);
F. Bowers Parker, Jr.: 160 (bottom);
Mr. and Mrs. Ralph L. Toon, Jr.: 18, 21, 27 (bottom).

Half-title page: Brick "cornerstone" from the Dr. Alfred M. Holloway house, Thomaston, Georgia.
Frontispiece: Alfred A. Kennedy house, Atlanta.
Table of Contents: Front elevation of the Montgomery-Portman house, Atlanta.

ISBN 0-932958-22-2
Library of Congress Catalog Card Number: 01–31862

Donors

Southern Architecture Foundation, Inc., (SAF) is a non-profit educational corporation located in Atlanta, Georgia. Established in April 1998, it is a tax-deductible public charity with 501(c)3 status. As we celebrate the publication of SAF's first book, *The Architecture of James Means,* we recognize and thank all whose cooperation and generosity have made it possible.

I.

The Julian T. and Grace L. Hightower Foundation, Inc.: in memory of Will and Anne Plowden, from their children
Harry Norman, Realtors
Mr. and Mrs. James K. Warren

II.

Amont Foundation, Inc.: Julie Purvis Montgomery and Arthur L. Montgomery
Mr. Louis N. Huff III: in memory of Jeannie Howard Huff
Mr. and Mrs. Harold Franklin McCart, Jr.
Mrs. D. Williams Parker
Mr. T. Marion Slaton
Mrs. Marguerite Neel Williams

III.

Mr. and Mrs. Norman D. Askins
Mr. and Mrs. James. W. Bland, Jr.
Mr. David Richmond Byers III (deceased)
Mr. and Mrs. E. Merrell Calhoun
Mr. and Mrs. Walker T. Candler
Mr. F. H. Boyd Coons
Mr. and Mrs. Frank C. Jones
Mrs. E. Buford King, Jr.
Mr. and Mrs. Larry Knox
Mrs. Thomas E. Martin, Jr.
Mr. and Mrs. C. Talbot Nunnally III
Mr. and Mrs. William A Parker, Jr
Sheffield Harrold Charitable Trust: Mr. and Mrs. Bradley Hale
Mr. and Mrs. Wesley Rhodes Vawter III
Young Friends of Southern Architecture Foundation, Inc.

IV.

Mr. and Mrs. Glenn Austin
Mr. and Mrs. William T. Baker
Mr. and Mrs. Dameron Black: in memory of David Richmond Byers III
Mrs. Belle Turner Cross
Mr. and Mrs. J. Christopher Deisley
Judge and Mrs. William H. Dender
Mr. Washington Dender
Vivian and Sam DuBose
Mr. Donald L. Easterling
Mr. Julian T. Evans III
Mr. and Mrs. George W. Felker III
Mr. and Mrs. S. Taylor Glover
Mary E. Haverty Foundation, Inc.
Mr. and Mrs. F. Hamilton Kuhlke
Mr. and Mrs. A. Bradford Hodges
Mr. and Mrs. Van Jones Martin
Mr. William R. Mitchell, Jr.: in memory of David Richmond Byers III
Miss Anne Morgan Moore
Mr. and Mrs. Arthur W. Rollins
Mr. and Mrs. Robert P. Shapard III
Mr. and Mrs. John G. Stewart
Mr. and Mrs. Ralph L. Toon, Jr.
Mr. and Mrs. Samuel M. Torrence
Mr. and Mrs. Phil Walden
Mr. and Mrs. William C. Warren III
Dr. and Mrs. J. Herbert West
Williams Family Foundation of Georgia, Inc.
Mr. and Mrs. Thomas M. Willingham

V.

Mr. Thomas E. Addison III: in memory of David Richmond Byers III
Miss Nancy Ager
Mrs. McCary Ballard
Mr. and Mrs. James C. Braithwaite
Dr. and Mrs. Arthur B. Chandler, Jr.
Mrs. James E. Clark
Cronk Duch & Miller, Architects
Dr. and Mrs. James B. Dunaway
Mr. and Mrs. Edward P. Ellis
Dr. and Mrs. Thomas J. Florence
Mr. Kenneth Garcia, Jr.
Mr. John T. Glover
Mr. and Mrs. Charles Harrison
Mr. and Mrs. Rawson Haverty
Kathy Barnes Hendricks
Mrs. John D. Hightower
Historical Concepts, Inc.
Dr. and Mrs. Alfred M. Holloway
Mr. and Mrs. Henry L. Howell
Mr. and Mrs. William E. Huger III
Mr. George H. Lanier
Mr. and Mrs. James R. Lockhart
Mr. and Mrs. Jeremiah Luxemburger
Mr. Steven L. Markey
Mrs. M. Matthews Mitchell
Mrs. Frank C. Owens, Jr.
Mr. Jared Paul
Mr. and Mrs. John C. Portman III
Mr. Neel W. Reid
H. English and Ermine Cater Robinson Foundation, Inc.
Mr. D. Jack Sawyer and Dr. William E. Torres
Mr. and Mrs. Mitchell F. Simmons
Mr. and Mrs. Frank O. Walsh III
Mrs. Joan Dobbs White
Mr. Tom B. Wight

VI.

Mr. and Mrs. J. Patrick Cline
Mr. and Mrs. James Cotton
Mrs. Matilda Martin Dobbs
Mrs. Norman Tee Faircloth
Joyce Mitchell Ferguson
Mr. William A. Fickling, Jr.
Mrs. James N. Frazer
Mr. and Mrs. Edward Hudson
Dr. Sidney Isenberg
Mr. L. Comer Jennings
Macon Town Committee, Colonial Dames of America
Mr. and Mrs. Frank A. Maier, Jr.
Mr. and Mrs. Reynolds McClatchey
Mr. and Mrs. Roy W. Mann, Jr.
Mr. and Mrs. E. Fay Pearce
Pinetree Garden Club
Miss Meredith Reid
Jane Powers Weldon
Mrs. Thomas W. Ventulett
Vinings Woman's Club

Contents

Preface, Acknowledgments, and Dedication

I was introduced to the architecture of James Means in 1958 (during my sophomore year in college) in the form of a house being built in Griffin, Georgia, on College Street. It was designed in the eighteenth-century Williamsburg, Virginia, style, and I had passed it several times while it was under construction as I drove south from Atlanta to Macon, Georgia, before the days of I-75. That was forty years before we incorporated Southern Architecture Foundation in April 1998 and conceived this book as our initial project. It is the foundation's first, and my fifteenth, book.

I had first visited the Colonial Williamsburg Restoration the year before, in June 1957, so it was a very pleasant surprise to find an extraordinarily fine version of the George Wythe house in plain view as I drove my mother to Macon. We generally took that route to enjoy the sights of that beautiful residential street, graced with many good examples of nineteenth- and early twentieth-century domestic architecture. Some forty years later College Street is still the center of a charming neighborhood, and James Means's Williamsburg-style beauty remains one of the street's architectural landmarks. But there is more to the story.

On one of our trips south that year, I noticed that the Griffin version of Williamsburg's Wythe house was clearly about finished; there were workmen's trucks parked around, so I stopped in front. I wanted to go inside because architecture is more than façades or front elevations, important as those faces presented to the world may be. I told my mother it was probably now or never to see it. But she wouldn't explore with me, "intrude." She would wait in the car.

Gingerly, I entered the unlocked front door, and, as luck would have it, Anne Plowden was coming down the stairs, looking elegant and intrigued by a college student's enthusiasm for her new Jimmy Means house, which she and her husband, Will Best Plowden, and young children had not yet occupied. It was being finished and furnished.

Anne Hightower Plowden was gracious, welcoming, and informative, and she took me on the fifty-cent tour. In 1958 that bought a great deal more than a quick glimpse. I recall commenting on some of the stylish furnishings already in place, one antique mahogany table in particular. She said that it was a gift for the house from her mother. I learned later that her mother was Mrs. Julian (Grace) Hightower of Thomaston, Georgia, whose own beautifully furnished home was designed by Philip Shutze, assisted by James Means, and built in 1948–49. (Later, in 1982, I featured it in *Landmark Homes of Georgia.*)

Mrs. Plowden talked about the marvel of Jimmy Means (which many of his clients and friends called him), how knowledgeable he was, designing and then overseeing every detail of construction ("such beautiful woodwork") and landscaping; how he helped find seasoned building materials, such as old bricks and heart pine. She commented that he was certainly an experienced artist who expressed and built an understated, well-studied ideal of historical beauty during an era when one-story ranch houses with picture windows were becoming the suburban norm. Means was keeping alive the classical tradition, giving life to bricks and mortar, wood, plaster and paint, authentic period style, details and craft, geometry, scale, proportion, and plan. It was normal for him to help chose sites and educate clients, traveling with them as well as steering them toward places for inspiration for their own homes. He became a friend and introduced them to other clients, who formed a coterie of Means enthusiasts.

Visiting this new Plowden place was part of my own education. It was clear that if one had the motivation, patience, and purse, James Means of Atlanta could make a dream house come true. Obviously, the Plowden house made an unforgettable impression on me and was a splendid first introduction to the subject of our book.

Prefaces are for scholars to cite influences and acknowledge sources and individuals—where an author's knowledge and motivation come from to write the book: who is writing and why (how does he know?). Clearly this book evolves from many years of appreciation and study of the architecture of historical traditionalists like James Means. The Plowden house was an eye opener. (After all, architecture is one of the visual arts.)

My second encounter with the architecture of James Means came in 1966, when a group of old-house enthusiasts in Washington-Wilkes, Georgia, began to search for important examples of vernacular architecture in that area, which had been settled in the 1770s. Included in the group were Osborne Bounds Jr., Dr. Turner Bryson, and me. Osborne was preparing to have Means create a new house for him, moving to a new site an abandoned, circa-1820, plantation-plain-style dwelling found near Washington-Wilkes and using parts, also, from two other derelict old houses from the area. The group saw all three of the houses, and the finished Means restoration assemblage was accomplished in 1968. I did not meet Means at this time, but I certainly heard Osborne's praise of his architect's skill, taste, and quiet perseverance. (See page 98 for the results.)

I finally met Jimmy Means in January 1970 at the initial meeting of the Tullie Smith House Restoration Committee of the Atlanta Historical Society, on which we had been asked to serve. The committee would be restoring an antebellum plantation-plain-style farmhouse that had been moved from a congested site in metropolitan Atlanta to the grounds of the historical society.

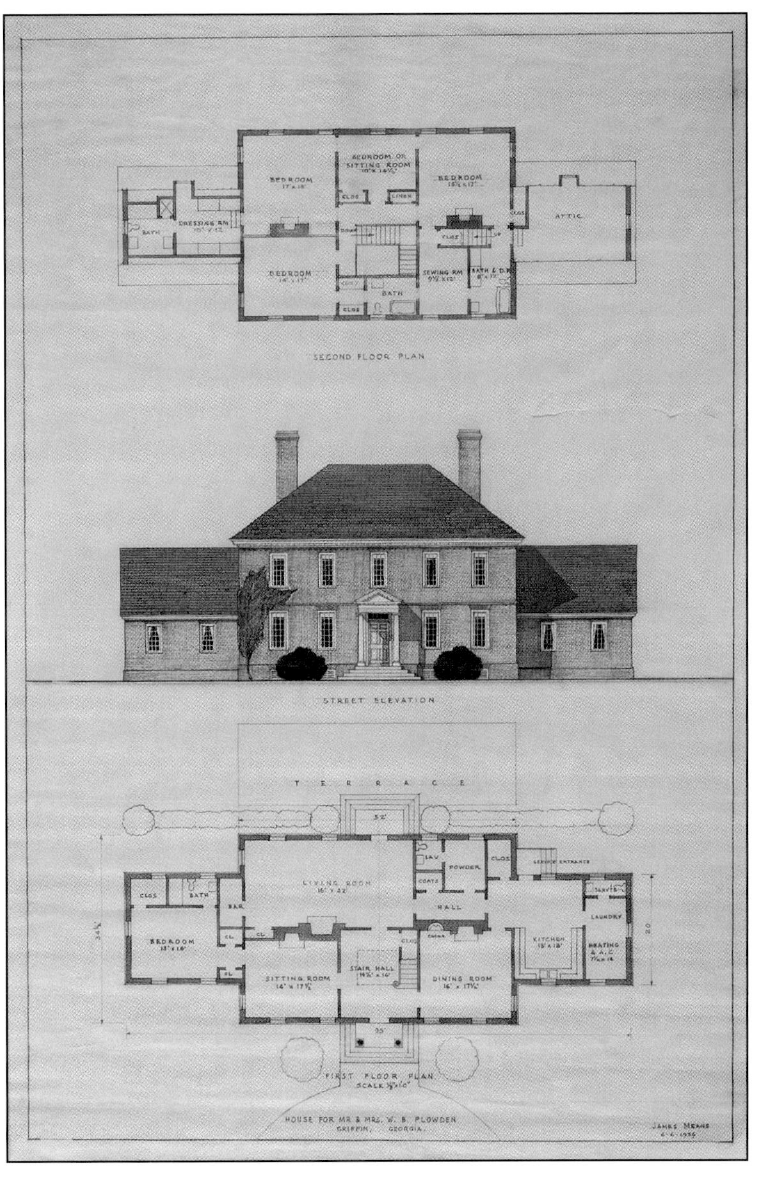

Means's elevation and plans for the Plowden house in Griffin, Georgia. The inspiration for the central block of the Plowden house, especially the rear elevation (see page 39), was the George Wythe house (mid-1750s) in Williamsburg, Virginia.

I was director at that time of the Georgia historic sites survey of the Georgia Historical Commission, the state historic preservation agency. Among my duties with the state was preparing detailed nominations for the National Register of Historic Places, which I did for the Tullie Smith House after its restoration. Because Means had been in charge of the Stone Mountain plantation restoration (see page 27) in the early 1960s, he had been asked to do some preliminary conjectural drawings for the house prior to the committee's inaugural meeting. Only one of these drawings has survived in the Means Collection at the Atlanta Historical Society, a collection vital to the creation of this book. At that meeting I was asked to direct the research and restoration of the 1840s house. Thereafter Means and I had lunch from time to time, and I went by his small office behind Kenneth Garcia's antique shop in an old house on East Paces Ferry Road in the Buckhead section of Atlanta to look over his architectural library, talk shop, and enjoy his interesting, old-fashioned office dominated by a drafting table. He even lent me a book or two from his extensive library, which was strong in Americana. One book in particular was part XII of *The Georgian Period, Measured Drawings of Colonial Work* (1902), containing numerous photographs of Savannah and other Georgia and Southern locations. I still have a photocopy of that section of the rare volume.

About that time the Middle Georgia Historical Society was seeking a National Register nomination for a house built in 1926 in Macon, Georgia: the so-called Villa Albicini, the Daniel Horgan house, an Italian baroque–style pavilion across from the Wesleyan College campus. Although it was fewer than fifty years old, the normal minimum for registration, it was exceptional enough to qualify—if that exceptional status could be well established. James Means had been the draftsman for this Hentz, Reid & Adler design, signing the drawings JM, as was his custom. It was during the time that he would later be described as having served as "Neel Reid's hands," Neel Reid being the firm's chief designer and Means's mentor.

The historical society attributed the design of the Horgan house entirely to Reid, who grew up and started his architectural career there in Macon. (Neel Reid was a local hero, a warranted status.) I thought that Philip Shutze probably had had something to do with the design, since it occurred at the time Reid was ailing with a brain tumor, about the time, in fact, that Reid died in the winter of 1926.

Since Means was Reid's hands and the drawings showed Means's initials, I had lunch with Jimmy Means to discuss what he remembered about that project. The question was authorship: did Neel Reid design the house for his longtime clients, the Horgans, or was the designer some other member of the firm of Hentz, Reid & Adler? Means and I dined at the Hickory House, a barbeque restaurant then located on Pharr Road near his office. It seemed a natural place for two Georgia boys to share lunch, even though we were discussing a subject perhaps more esoteric than brunswick stew.

The Horgan project had occurred forty-five years earlier, in 1971. Jimmy, in his direct and understated manner, recalled that he had been the draftsman, but he believed that "the firm" had designed the house, "no one person." He considered Philip Shutze's contribution to have been "a trunk of photographs of Italian subjects" that Shutze had brought back with him from his days at the American Academy in Rome, Italy, before and after World War I.

Armed with that amplifying firsthand information, I was able to register the beautiful little Horgan villa for the Middle Georgia Historical Society, even if it was less than the minimum half-century old. More important, it was for me the beginnings of a lifelong quest to understand what I have called the Georgia school of classicists. (See Appendix II.)

As a result of Jimmy Means's and my acquaintance on the Tullie Smith House committee, in the early 1970s he invited me to call on some of his clients, including Dr. and Mrs. Sanders Pike (page 90) and Virginia Campbell Courts, whose house he had renovated at 24 Cherokee Road in the Buckhead residential area. He also introduced me to Philip Shutze, whose assistant he had become after Neel Reid's death, and I met his daughter, Mary Catherine Means, when she was a teenager and he and Mr. Shutze were attending a lecture at the Atlanta Historical Society. On that occasion Jimmy asked me to talk with Mary Catherine about a career in historic preservation, which she was interested in pursuing (and did, quite successfully, at a national level). Mary Catherine has been a great help with this book, of course, and she has been a member of the board of Southern Architecture Foundation since early after its incorporation in 1998.

Another original board member of SAF, Inc., was the late designer and interiors consultant David Richmond Byers III, longtime vice president of Atlanta's W. E. Browne Decorating Company, who died in August 1998. David Byers worked closely with Means on many projects, understood his importance, and was a source of enlightenment for me. David was a friend and mentor of mine for thirty years, opening doors for me into the world of the Georgia classicists, especially that of Edward Vason Jones (1909–80), with whom David worked closely on White House and U.S. State Department projects. With Edward Jones, in 1951 Means formed a partnership, Jones & Means, which lasted only about two years, brought to a close largely because of the illness of Means's only son, who would die of cancer in 1956.

My *Edward Vason Jones, Architect, Connoisseur, and Collector* (1995) describes the association of Means and Jones, who had first become acquainted in the late 1930s when they both were with Hentz, Adler & Shutze, the successor firm to Hentz, Reid & Adler. David Byers, James Means, and Edward Vason Jones were important colleagues in the Georgia school of classicists. That I knew them all has been a great help with this book.

When Mrs. Ray (Callie) Efird, Mary Catherine Means, and Mrs. Ralph (Nancy) Toon published a memorial tribute to Means, *The Houses of James Means*, in 1979, after Means's death, David Byers presented me with a copy, which has been a great resource in this book project. It is practically destroyed from constant use. Fortunately, I have two others, and Nancy Toon gave me two of the original dust jackets to improve the appearance of my worn copies. (David Byers left me his own copy when he died.)

Callie Huger Efird and I worked together in 1971 on an article for the High Museum of Art Antiques Show catalogue about my work for the Georgia Historical Commission historic sites survey. We conferred many times in her Jimmy Means house on Atlanta's Valley Road, and we discussed Means's unique architectural career and contributions. Later, when Van Jones Martin and I produced *Classic Atlanta* in 1991, we included this Efird House of 1965. Callie Efird has since died, and the house was sold, but we have used here Martin's photographs of the place taken in 1989 for the earlier book, showing the house as it appeared during the Efirds' ownership and as I knew it first in 1971. (See page 14).

When Van Martin and I produced *Landmark Homes of Georgia* in 1982, we included Peggy and Tom Martin's beautiful Tidewater Virginia–inspired Means house in Atlanta. (David Byers helped Peggy Martin with interior decoration.) I featured Means's career with that important house, and here we have reused those Van Martin photographs because they captured perfectly one of Means's largest private commissions, which has changed very little since it was built in 1965. (His largest commission was for the Georgia Stone Mountain Authority in the early 1960s: finding, moving, and reassembling seventeen antique buildings from around Georgia to create a facsimile plantation complex at Stone Mountain Park.)

For the March/April 1989 issue of *Southern Homes* magazine, I wrote an article, "The Architecture of James Means, Georgia Classicist," about four Means houses, two from the late 1950s and two from the mid-1960s. At that time these were the homes of their original owners, Nancy MacDougald, the Roy Dorseys, the William Parkers, and the Walter Blooms. In this article I wrote, "Means'[s] houses are the culmination of more than 70 years of Georgia classicism growing out of the firm begun by Hal Hentz and Neel Reid, a tradition carried forward by Philip Shutze, and then enriched by Means after the firm ceased to exist." The title of that magazine article has become the title of this book.

The book's specific origin was a conversation I had with James K. (Jimmy) Warren in early 1998 soon after the publication of my *J. Neel Reid, Architect, of Hentz, Reid & Adler, and the Georgia School of Classicists* (1997). It took place in Jimmy and Rebekah Warrens' James Means house completed in 1974 as the home of Mr. and Mrs. William A. Rooker, Jr. in Cobb County, Georgia, near Vinings. The Warrens' first child, their daughter, Charlotte, was less than a year old. Also present were Rebekah's parents, Martha and Reynolds McClatchey, who are members of a study club for which I had recently given a slide lecture based on my Reid book. Jimmy Warren knew that Means had been a Reid protege. He proposed that my next book project be a new Means book to follow the Reid volume, which I had done in conjunction with the Georgia Trust for Historic Preservation, of which I had been a founding trustee in 1973.

Jimmy Warren and I decided to incorporate Southern Architecture Foundation as a 501(c)3 educational charity with this book as its founding project and initial fund-raiser. Because the Reid book was beginning to show promise as a successful Georgia Trust fund-raiser, leading to a Georgia Trust Neel Reid travel fellowship, this plan seemed feasible for SAF, Inc. Jimmy Warren's philanthropy and interest in entrepreneurial development made the legal costs of the incorporation and IRS registration possible, and his support and youthful enthusiasm have helped to make both the foundation and this first project a reality.

Jimmy Warren and Martha McClatchey were taking my Evening at Emory continuing education course, Atlanta Architecture and Historic Preservation, in the winter of 1998 when we dreamed up this book project. Martha became SAF's first registrar, helping Jimmy and me identify all current owners of the Means houses. In this effort we were assisted by the 1985 revised edition of the 1979 *The Houses of James Means*, which had made that information current for the six years that had passed since the first edition. (Both editions were American Cancer Society fund-raisers, honoring Means and his late son, James Jr., who had died of cancer in 1956 when he was ten-and-a-half years old.)

Ownership, of course, is a constantly changing matter, so it is impossible for a publication ever to have the last word on that aspect. Many of these owners, original and current, have contributed to the cost of this publication and thus to the establishment of SAF, which will recycle the proceeds toward other foundation projects. The contributors are listed in the front of the book, and some are especially acknowledged below for help in research.

Southern Architecture Foundation has had a series of promotional events during the creation of this book; each has been held in a different Means house: the first was in November 1998 at the home of the James Warrens (the third owners), the second was at the home of the Walker Candlers (the second owners), and the third was at the home of the Ralph Toons, who worked with Means to create their home in 1971–72. These events have helped to call firsthand attention to Means's architecture. James Means's daughter, Mary Catherine, now of Alexandria, Virginia, attended the first event, each of which has been a highly successful way of focusing attention on this undertaking.

Among the people whose help I want to single out here are all Means house owners, past and present; all the SAF board members and the SAF executive committee, committee chairman Marion Slaton, me, Jimmy Warren, and Boyd Coons (who has helped me produce the SAF newsletter, *The Piazza*); James Lockhart for his expert photography and cheerful help in locating current owners of Means houses; and Van Jones Martin of Golden Coast Publishing Company, Savannah, an SAF board member and invaluable contributor to the publishing and creative process. Especially tedious and technical was Lockhart's work in copying Means's drawings at the Atlanta History Center, which he did with care and perfection. Lockhart, Martin, and I have collaborated on several other books, including *Classic New Orleans* (1992) and *J. Neel Reid, Architect* (1997). Mrs. Mary Mangham Means, now in her nineties, was helpful with biographical details about her former husband's life and career. Kenneth H. Thomas, Jr., historian of the State Historic Preservation Division and much-published genealogist, has provided invaluable help with Means's genealogy, unearthing data previously unknown. (Mary Catherine Means was delighted.) I want to acknowledge the patient assistance of the staff of the Atlanta History Center during research and photographic copy work on the Means materials that Mary Catherine Means has placed there as part of their permanent architectural archives.

In the years since Means's death and the publication of *The Houses of James Means*, both in 1979, our perspective on the significance and quality of his life and architecture has deepened. There has been a growing interest in the classical tradition and traditional architecture. (See Sources, page 176.) In SAF's book, we have published more color, more plans and drawings, and newly discovered works and data that were not available for the 1979 book. Among those people not already mentioned who have been especially helpful were Laura Hagler, Elaine Luxemburger, Norman Askins and his staff, millwork specialist Jim Girdler, and the late architect Linton H. Young, who knew Means when they were both teenagers. SAF sees Means—Georgia born and Georgia trained—as a fine example of an architect in the South who continued traditions from the South in his architecture; he is our inaugural muse.

Last I must thank once again my mother, Miriam Hays Mitchell, now in her nineties, whom I mentioned in the opening paragraphs of this prefatory essay. She was with me in 1958 when I was introduced to Means's architecture and, thankfully, still is as I write this preface more than forty years later. I dedicate this book to her and to a baker's dozen other Southern ladies, without whom I couldn't have completed this project:

Belle Turner Cross
Callie Huger Efird (d. 1994)
Laura Plowden Hagler
Rebecca Hardaway King
Martha Hightower McClatchey
Peggy Sheffield Martin
Mary Catherine Means
Julie Purvis Montgomery
Diane Williams Parker
Mary Lynne Smith
Nancy Thompson Toon
Jane Powers Weldon
Marguerite Neel Williams (d. 1999)

William R. Mitchell, Jr.
26 February 2001
President, The History Business, LLC
President, Southern Architecture Foundation, Inc.

Chronology

Photographic portrait of James Collier Means (at right) with his siblings, about 1909. From Jimmy, clockwise, William, John, and Embree.

Below: In 1927 Means drew the morning room column details for the Edward H. Inman ("Swan") House in Atlanta for Hentz, Reid & Adler.

1840s John Means, grandfather of James Means, founded Meansville, in Pike County, Georgia, about forty miles south of Atlanta.

1904 August 27, James Collier Means was born at Indian Springs, Georgia (between Atlanta and Macon).

1906 The Means family moved to Atlanta, to the West End neighborhood, where Jimmy's father, John F. Means, established a contracting business.

1917 Jimmy Means took a job as a part-time office boy with the architectural firm of Hentz, Reid & Adler. (Mrs. Means knew Hal Hentz's in-laws, the Connallys, prominent West End neighbors.)

1919 A teenager of fifteen, Means began drafting for Hentz, Reid & Adler, signing drawings "JM," while a student at Tech High School.

1921 Means was graduated from Tech High. Still drafting at Hentz, Reid & Adler, he began studies in architecture at Georgia Tech, but soon decided he preferred full-time employment as a draftsman.

1926 Neel Reid, chief designer for Hentz, Reid & Adler, died February 14 at age forty. Means was later described as having been "Reid's hands" during the noted architect's struggle with the effects of brain cancer.

1927 January 1, Hentz, Reid & Adler became Hentz, Adler & Shutze; Philip Shutze replaced Neel Reid as the firm's principal designer.

Mid-1930s During the Depression, Means took a Federal position in Washington, D.C., designing post offices.

1941 James Collier Means married Mary Mangham, a nurse; they had three children in the 1940s: Mary Catherine, 1944; James Collier, Jr., 1945; and Sarah Anita (Sally), 1947.

c. 1942–43 Means worked with post engineering at Fort MacPherson, Georgia, in military service.

1944–45 Hentz, Adler & Shutze became Shutze, Armstead & Adler, then Shutze & Armstead. Means continued with the firm.

1950 Philip Shutze began to practice alone, with Means as an associate. There was little work in the office.

Below: House for E. Frank Pharr.

1951 Means hung out his shingle as a residential designer, designing the E. Frank Pharr house at 420 Argonne Drive, in Atlanta.

Means converted a screened porch to a formal library and designed a garden entrance doorway for Richard Sawtell's 1922 Atlanta house designed by Hentz, Reid & Adler.

1952 Means formed a partnership, Jones & Means, with Edward Vason Jones of Albany, Georgia, a former Hentz, Reid & Adler associate. Means moved his wife and three small children to Albany.

1953 Jones & Means designed the Angus Alberson house in Albany.

1954 Ed Jones and Jimmy Means dissolved their partnership, with Means taking any work and clients north of Macon back with him to Atlanta, where he practiced residential architecture alone until his death in 1979.

The first project for Means's practice back in Atlanta was for Arthur L. Montgomery, originally a Jones & Means client.

"I came across a good drawing of "D'Evereux" in Natchez, in the second volume of Great Georgian Houses of America *and have been influenced by it to alter my proportions somewhat. Still holding basically to our accepted design. I have increased the cupola to 10 ft. sq. (added 1 ft.) raised the columns of the portico on a 7" curb above the floor (like D'Evereux), lowered the height of the columns and decreased the size of the entablature to 4'0." The whole proportion of the house is improved by these changes."*

Signed Jimmy Means, January 14, 1946, to Edward Vason Jones, regarding the Robert W. Groves house, completed in 1948, near Savannah, Georgia, a Jones and Means collaboration about five years before they were officially partners in Jones & Means.

Above: Jimmy Means with his children (from left): Sarah Anita (Sally), Mary Catherine, and James Jr.

Angus Alberson house, Albany.

Following is a list of Means houses and projects arranged by completion dates; clients are listed alphabetically when more than one were completed in a single year.

1957	Ager, Mrs. Mary-Lucille; Atlanta. Daniel project; Greenville, South Carolina (with Philip Shutze). Ellis, William; Lake Lanier, Georgia.
1958	Cook, Marcus; Atlanta. Courts, Richard; Atlanta (remodeling). Jones, Jesse; Cornelia, Georgia. Plowden, Will; Griffin, Georgia.

Clockwise, from above: Philip Shutze and Jimmy Means at the Daniel house, Greenville, S.C. House for Jesse Jones, Cornelia, Georgia. House for Mr. and Mrs. J. Ray Efird, Atlanta. House for William Appleby, Atlanta. Postcard view of the plantation complex at Stone Mountain, near Atlanta.

1959	Bloom, Dr. Walter; Marietta, Georgia. Dorsey, Roy; Atlanta.
1961	Hedges, Mrs. James; Lookout Mountain, Dade County, Georgia
1962	Hightower, Julian; Thomaston, Georgia (addition, with Philip Shutze).
1963	Davenport, J. H.; Chattanooga (Lookout Mountain), Tennessee. Dender, Judge William; Etowah, Tennessee. Haverty, Rawson; Atlanta. Shackelford, Francis; Atlanta. Stone Mountain Plantation; Atlanta vicinity.
1964	Ballard, McCary; Atlanta. Barrett, Mrs. H. Gould; Augusta, Georgia. Bryant, Dr. Milton; Atlanta. Ellis, Dr. John; Atlanta. Felker, George III; Monroe, Georgia. MacDougald, Nancy; Atlanta.
1965	Appleby, William; Atlanta. Efird, J. Ray; Atlanta. Parker, William A., Jr.; Atlanta.
1966	Martin, Thomas; Atlanta.

1966 Pike, Dr. Sanders; Marietta, Georgia.
Tarrymore preliminary project design; Atlanta.
Torrence, Samuel; Dothan, Alabama.

1968 Bounds, Osborne; Washington-Wilkes, Georgia.
Stewart, John; Gastonia, North Carolina.

1969 Shapard, Robert; Griffin, Georgia.

1970 Browne, Dr. Harry; Nashville, Tennessee.
Milner, Gene; Atlanta.
Smith, Tullie; Atlanta
(restoration, proposal unexecuted).

Above: House for Dr. Harry G. Browne, Nashville, Tennessee.
Left: House for Jack Carr, Montgomery, Alabama.
Below: House for William Akers, Nashville, Tennessee.
Bottom: Gazebo for Dr. Thomas Florence, Marietta, Georgia; now on the grounds of the Atlanta History Center.

1971 Carr, Jack; Montgomery, Alabama.
Erwin-Maynard house; Atlanta (moved and renovated for a cousin of Philip Shutze).
Moore, Dr. B. Waldo; Atlanta.

1972 Cartee, Terry; Crawfordville, Georgia.
Florence, Dr. Thomas; Marietta, Georgia.
Forbes and Rayburn; near Marshallville, Georgia.
Toon, Ralph; Atlanta.

1973 Kleiner, Dr. Jack; Atlanta.

1974 Coxe, Tench; Atlanta.
Kennedy, Alfred; Atlanta.
Rooker, William; Atlanta (Cobb County).

1975 Akers, William; Nashville, Tennessee.
Hennessy, Robert; Atlanta.

1976 Cavender, Ralph; Claxton, Georgia.
Parker, Bowers; near Scottsboro, Alabama.

1977 Holloway, Dr. Alfred; Thomaston, Georgia.

1978 West, Dr. J. Herbert; Alpharetta vicinity, Georgia.

1979 Anderburg-Huff, Atlanta (1979–80).

February 8, James Collier Means died as a result of injuries suffered in an automobile crash.

The Houses of James Means was published.

1998 Southern Architecture Foundation was incorporated, with *The Architecture of James Means, Georgia Classicist*, as its initial project.

Introduction

James Collier Means (1904–79), known simply as Jimmy, was a Georgia architect of the "old school"; he was a steadfast classicist when the suburban ranch house, with a streamlined Ford in the carport, had become an ideal for a postwar futuristic world. Commenting on a modern new church building with an oddly angled metallic steeple, Means remarked characteristically to a client, "That church is unnecessarily ugly." This droll and definitive way of speaking endeared him to his clients, many of whom became his close friends, finding him and his work irresistible. His work was his life. (See Chronology, page 12).

Means and his clients loved the pre-expressway past. They took great pains, and pleasure, too, in breathing new life into the symmetrical beauties of eighteenth-century American and European styles, usually understated vernacular versions, and they preferred the comfortable "old shoes" of seasoned building materials, handcrafts, antique furnishings, and parterre gardens. Despite a changing society (or possibly because of it), this continuity seemed necessary and appropriate for life in modern America, especially in the South where Means was born and learned architecture as his profession.

He learned in the old-fashioned way, on the job, rather than in a college of architecture. His father, John Francis Means, was a versatile man, sometimes a newspaper editor and later a contractor. The family's roots were in middle Georgia in a town named for them, Meansville, which they had founded in the 1840s. The Meanses were talented people; one early relative was president of Emory College. Jimmy continued that tradition of versatility and talent, but his single-minded passion became designing and building houses that seemed like sparkling old homeplaces and the restoration of languishing houses that had once been flourishing centers of life.

Born, bred, and apprenticed in Georgia, where many of his designs are located, Means was only a young teenager (thirteen or fourteen) in Atlanta's West End, where his father settled in 1906, when he began to work part time as an office boy in 1917 with a premier Atlanta architectural firm, Hentz, Reid & Adler. By age fifteen he was drafting such things as roof plans and was on his way to becoming a card-carrying member of the Georgia school of classicists. (See Appendix II). At that time he was a high-school student studying mechanical drawing at Technical (Tech) High. (Jimmy's mother, Jessie Embree Means, knew Hal Hentz's mother-in-law, Mrs. Elijah L. Connally, of the Homestead in West End, who put in a good word for Jimmy at Hentz, Reid & Adler.)

At the end of his life, he would be the last of those still in practice to have worked with Neel Reid and Hal Hentz, the architects who founded the Georgia school after they returned home from studying architecture at Columbia University and European travel, to form Hentz & Reid in 1909. When Jimmy Means started out with the firm, another Columbia University–trained architect, Rudolph Adler, an Atlanta native, had just the year before been made a partner.

Means's career spanned from J. Neel Reid (1885–1926), his mentor, the firm's principal designer and tastemaker, through Philip Trammell Shutze (1890–1982; the firm became Hentz, Adler & Shutze in 1927), to Edward Vason Jones (1909–80). In 1952, after Philip Shutze retired during the Korean War (1950–53), Means and Edward Jones, his old colleague from Hentz, Adler & Shutze, formed Jones & Means at Albany, Georgia, Jones's hometown. Having married Mary Mangham in 1941, Means and his wife moved to Albany with their three young children, Mary (1944), James Jr. (1945), and Sally (1947). At that time Means was described in the *Albany Herald* as having been Reid's "hands," during the years when Reid gave up drafting before his death from brain cancer in 1926. (Ironically, that same form of cancer brought the Jones & Means partnership to an end after less than two years, and it launched a new phase in Means's career, when James Jr. was tragically diagnosed with it in the summer of 1954. To be near Emory University Hospital, the

Meanses returned to Atlanta in August, opening the door for his groundbreaking Arthur Montgomery project, during which the child died.)

Jimmy Means was one of the last of the master builders, the original meaning of architect. Not just capable of using the T-square, drafting paper, and pencil, he had also mastered the traditional tools of the carpenter-architect. Capable hands, indeed. He grounded his practice in the old ways of designing and building based in the human scale of the proportional systems of the classical orders and in enduring materials such as bricks, stone, and heart pine.

His credentials were based on his unique talents, experience, and knowledge rather than on registration with a state agency, and he was not a member of the American Institute of Architects. Means was a maverick, but a low-key, gentlemanly maverick. (The Maverick of Meansville?) He was an architect in the same way of Andrea Palladio, one of his Renaissance forebears, who learned from other architects and their designs, or, closer to home, in the way of Thomas Jefferson. As they had been, he was passionate about "well-building"; similarly, his natural talents and learning, his large library of architectural books, allowed him to build well. He was a professional because he was a perfectionist, and people were drawn to him and his work for that reason, allowing him to earn a modest living as an architect for his entire adult life. Everyone knew Jimmy Means was not in the profession for the money, but for the art.

Jimmy Means

The houses that Means designed and built from the early 1950s, when he returned to Atlanta from Albany and Jones & Means to practice alone, without draftsmen or secretary, are the culmination of more than seventy years of Georgia classicism growing out of Hentz, Reid & Adler and Hentz, Adler & Shutze. Means, his clients, contractors, masons, millworkers, and carpenters greatly enriched the tradition when few could still do it or afford it, or care. The following selection of a wide range of his works well demonstrates this enrichment. His first commission on his own in Atlanta, already mentioned, was a large French house for Arthur L. Montgomery and Montgomery's first wife, Eleanor Morgan. The Montgomerys were social, civic, and financial leaders; the Atlanta Coca-Cola Bottling Company was Montgomery's family enterprise. This beautiful custom-designed and fabricated house and generous client launched Means's career alone and helped to assure his reputation. Montgomery had grown up in a house designed by Hentz, Adler & Shutze and naturally chose as his architect one who had been associated with that firm. The Means house, which practically speaks for itself visually, follows on page 30.

One last word of introduction is necessary before we proceed. We can use the Montgomery house as an example of an instance where some explanation is required other than to say this was a Means design: from 1954 for Arthur Montgomery of a house completed in 1956, forty-five years ago.

During those decades, as with most all the houses in Selected Works, some changes have occurred, if the original owners are not still in residence and, sometimes even if they are. This house, as we go to press, has new owners, Mr. and Mrs. John (Jack and Erin) Portman III, who are the third owners since it was completed. Jack Portman is an architect in the internationally known Portman firm started by his father. He and his wife respect James Means's original conception, which is why they purchased it, but they want some necessary and desired renovations and additions, mainly in the rear rooms and on the terrace. He is making them judiciously and in keeping with the French provincial style that Means and the Montgomerys developed. James Lockhart's photographs depict the house as it exists today, three owners since 1956. It is clearly now the Montgomery-Portman house.

Similar stories can be told for many of the other thirty-three houses in Selected Works; very few are unchanged from their appearance when new, and most have changed hands several times since Means. My accompanying texts explain these changing aspects, all the while with an emphasis on the original conception and clients who commissioned our architect.

The conclusion also deals with some of these matters, twenty-two years after James Means's death in an automobile accident in the winter of 1979 and the publication of *The Houses of James Means* during the fall of that same year. The conclusion includes two houses that demonstrate how highly respected the Means legacy has been, the standards he set out for the future, even with major additions and renovations to the originals; those houses are a fine conclusion, indeed, to *The Architecture of James Means.*

Portfolio

"Jimmy Means was a unique person with a huge talent, a true artist, with an unfailing sense of proportion."

— William A. Parker Jr., Means client
21 December 1998

An impressive, natural-born draftsman, James Means (1904–79) began to draw for Hentz, Reid & Adler almost as soon as he began his association with the firm in 1917 as a part-time office boy. By 1919, when he was a student at Atlanta's Technical High School, and after graduation he was one of the firm's regular draftsmen, producing sheet after sheet of working drawings to be turned into blueprints and then into buildings. After Neel Reid ceased to draft in 1923 because of his cancer, Means was called Reid's hands. But Means was not just talented as an artist with pencil and pen; by apprenticeship he became a practical architect and an architectural scholar with a wide-ranging knowledge of historical precedents, American and European, vernacular and high style, to use in his own designs. Long after other architects had become modernists, he developed a virtuoso vocabulary of period styles in the manner of classic eclecticism. He also acquired a large working library of classic books and photographs, modeled on the extensive library at Hentz, Reid & Adler, later Hentz, Adler & Shutze, and even later, Shutze & Armstead.

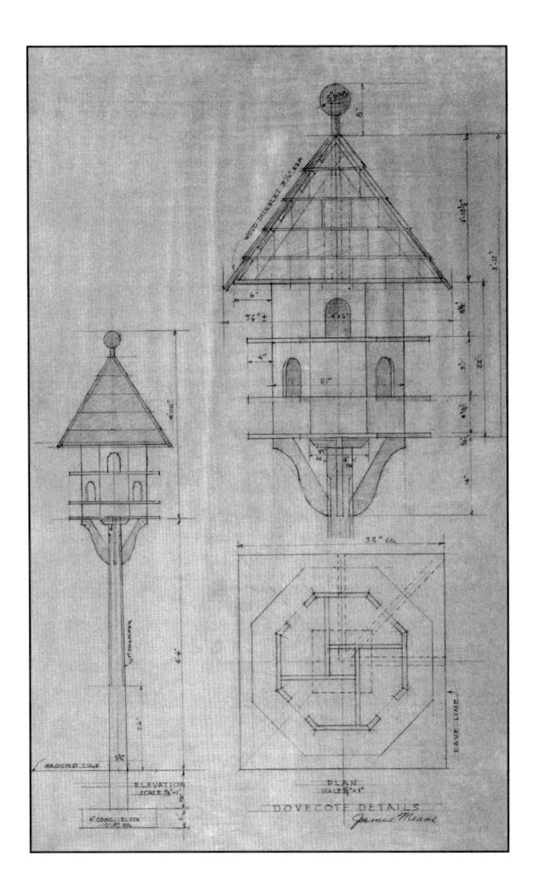

Dovecote details, client unknown.

At the turn of the century in which Means was born, practically all working drawings were made on architect's linen. This tedious discipline and process began with original drawings made on thin detail paper, then transferred with pens and India ink to the slick side of the linen. The entire process began with idea-sketches (*esquisses*) and then design proposals, sometimes in color, and renderings washed with color to give the client an idea of the proposed design and the finished building. Means's own renderings were almost always front elevation drawings in color, as he did for the Hedges house (page 27) and sometimes with floor plans at the bottom of the sheet, as he did for the Will Plowden house (page 9).

During the period just before World War I, when he began his office training, the ideal was that drawings as well as buildings should be works of art. This Portfolio illustrates Means's natural gift, which he perfected and practiced over his adult lifetime in architecture. One should remember also, that when Means returned to Atlanta from Albany to establish his practice, he worked alone. Every drawing, from preliminary sketches to the finished elevations and details, came from his hand. Throughout the book are details and entire designs, preliminary proposals, renderings, finished working drawings, floor plans, interior and exterior elevations, plot plans, landscapes and garden schemes. Most of these are previously unpublished. They come from both public and private collections, from family, friends, and clients. Seemingly, every scrap of James Means's graphic art has been treasured and saved.

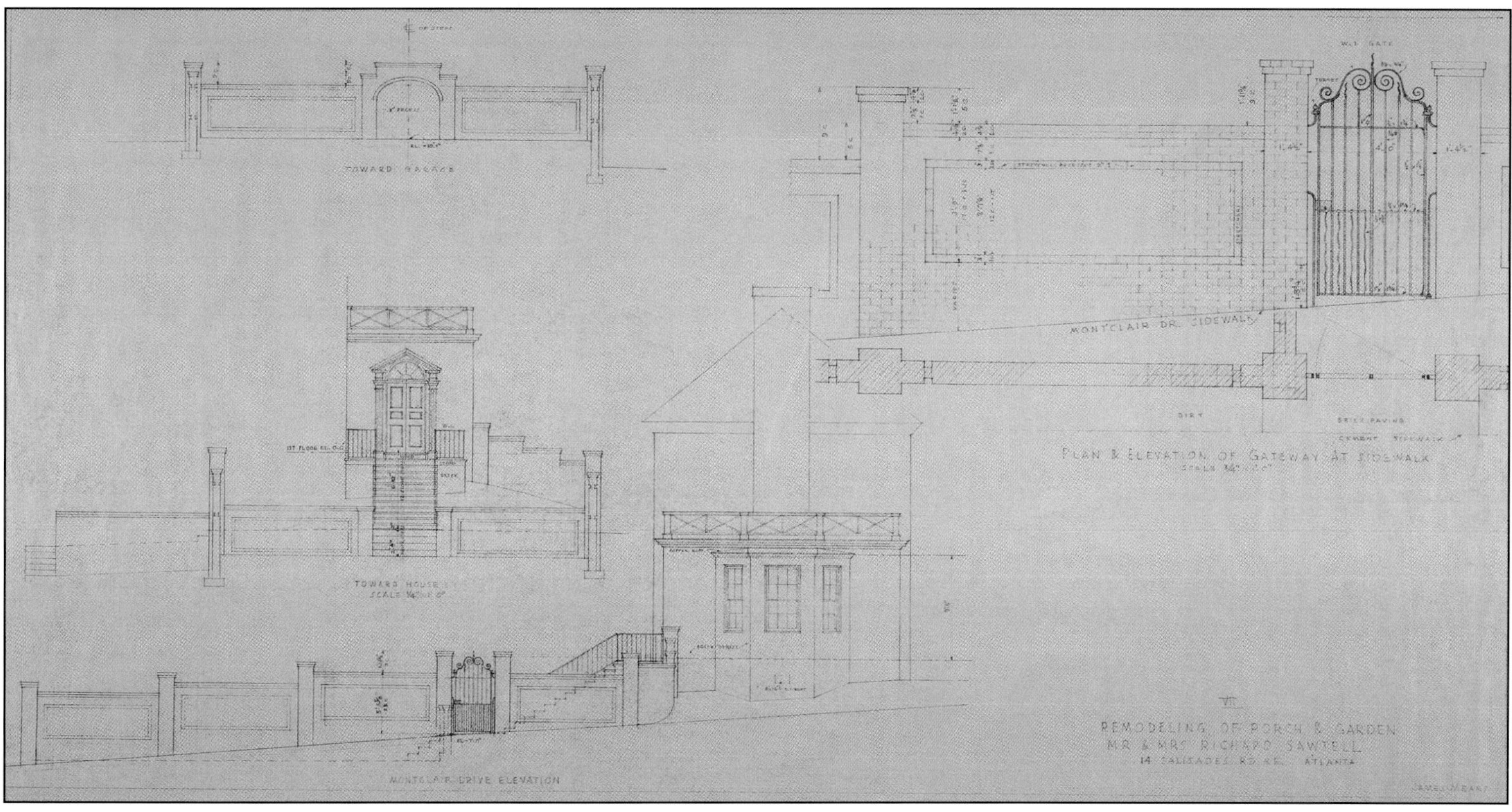

Two of Means's earliest designs from his own Atlanta commissions were the E. Frank Pharr house on Argonne Drive (top, see also page 13) and renovations and changes for Richard Sawtell in Brookwood Hills (above).

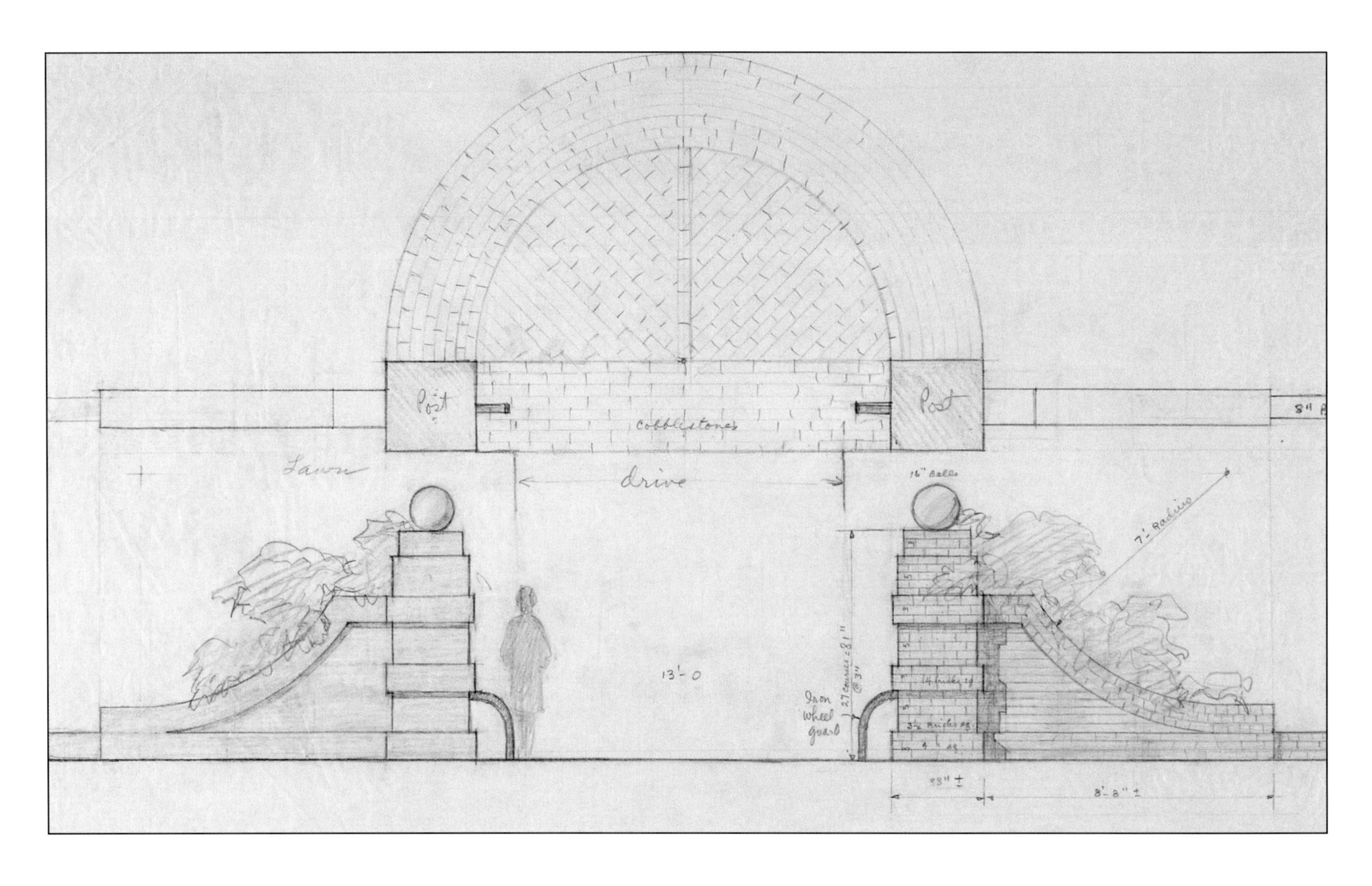

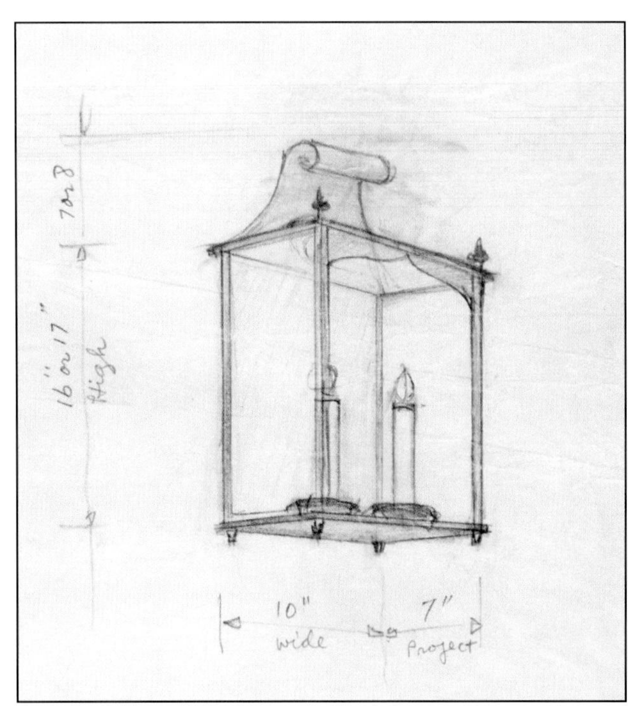

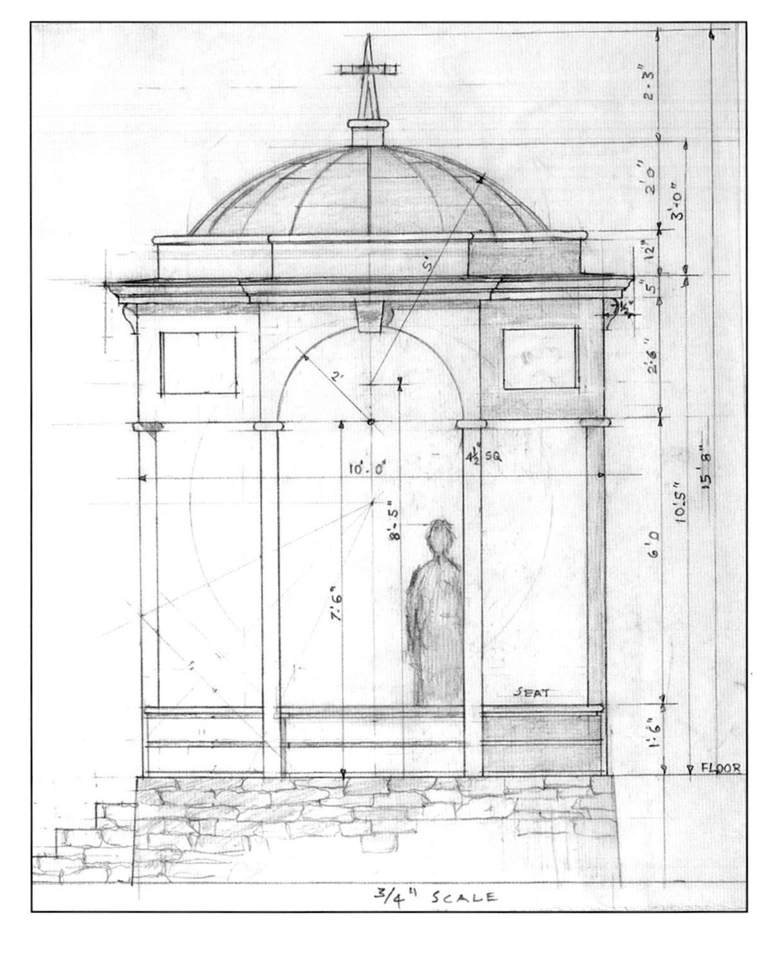

DETAILS
Top: Gate and forecourt design for Rawson Haverty house, Atlanta (see page 54). Above: Lantern for unidentified client. Right: Gazebo for Dr. Thomas Florence house, Marietta (see pages 15 and 122).

Means drawing of a two-story Williamsburg house showing the "lineaments," or controlling lines, classical architects used to produce a desired system of proportion.

Sketches.
Top: An unidentified three-part house.
Above left: Sketch based on Mulberry Plantation, in South Carolina.
Above right: Sketch of an Italianate villa.Right: Sketch based on Gunston Hall, Virginia.

Section sketch of a proposed church shows Means planning interiors as part of the overall composition.

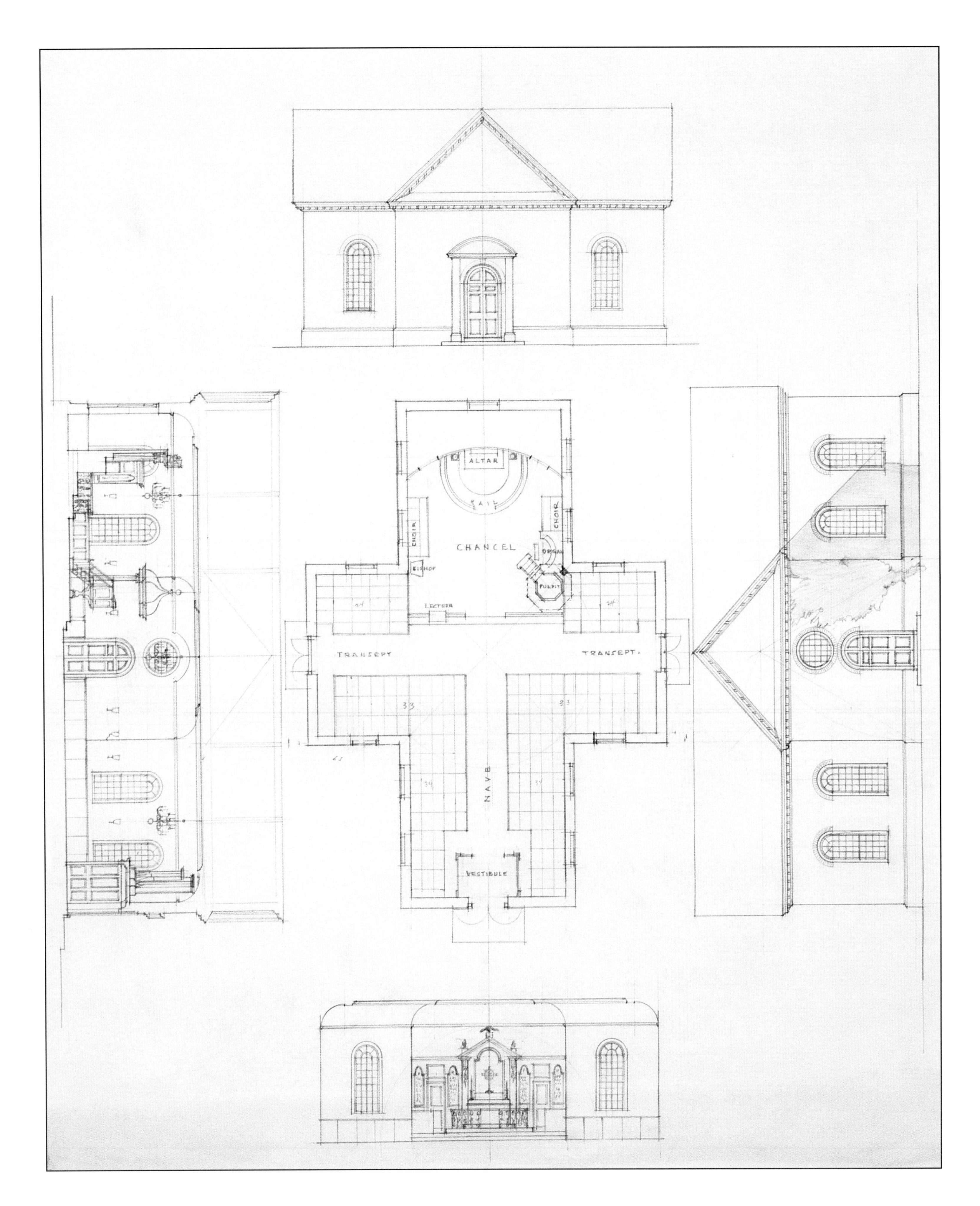
ALTAR
RAIL
CHOIR
CHOIR
CHANCEL
ORGAN
BISHOP
PULPIT
LECTERN
TRANSEPT
TRANSEPT
NAVE
VESTIBULE

INTERIOR DESIGN
Above: Rendering of living room for the Waldo Moore house (page 118). Below: Rendering of paneled room for Dr. Thomas Florence. Opposite page: Means's drawing of a church similar to Christ Church in Lancaster County, Virginia, again shows interior planning as part of a comprehensive design concept.

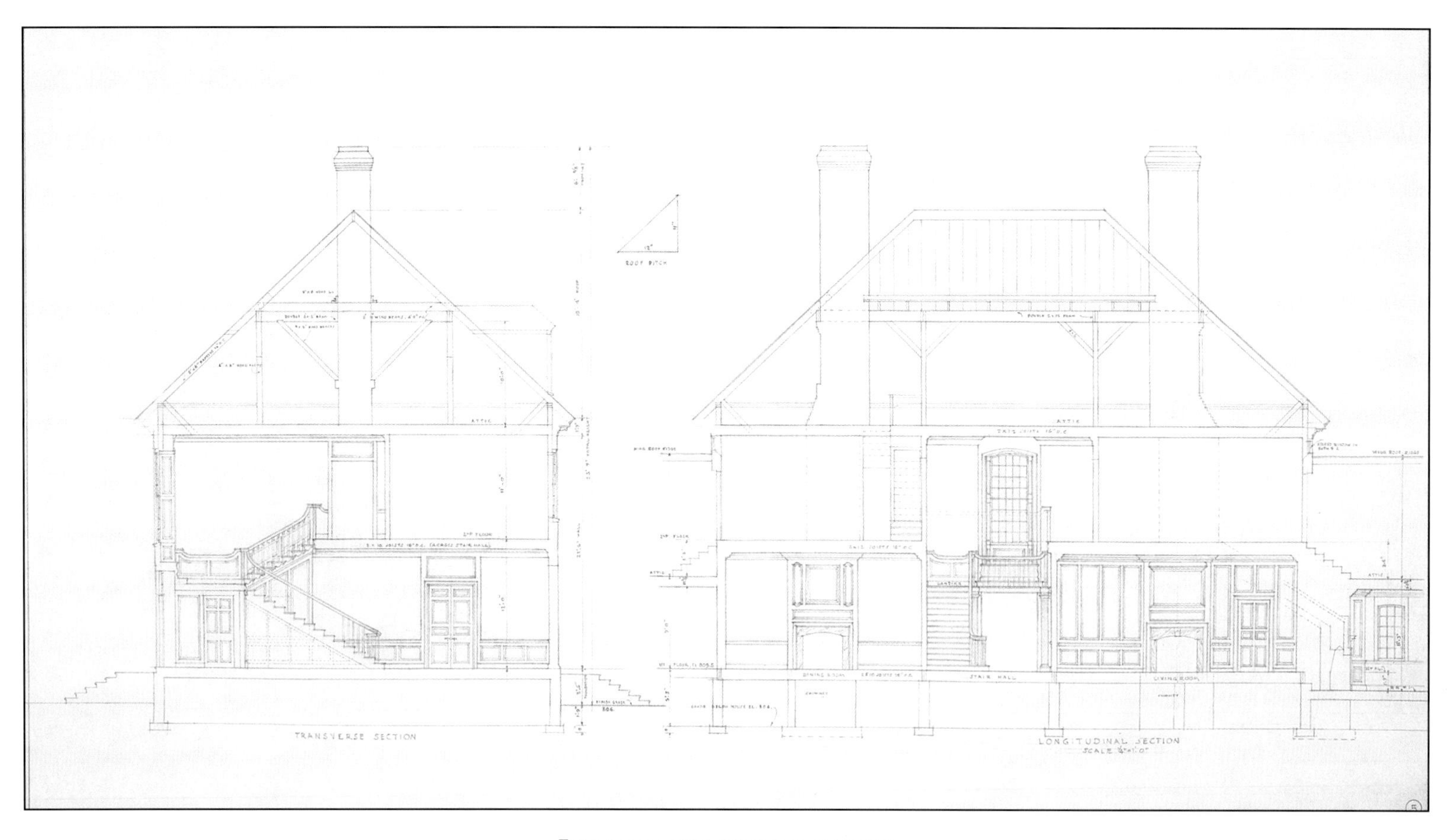

ELEVATIONS WITH INTERIOR SECTIONS
Above: Thomas Martin house.
DETAIL ELEVATIONS
Below: Entrance and window details from the Marcus Cook house

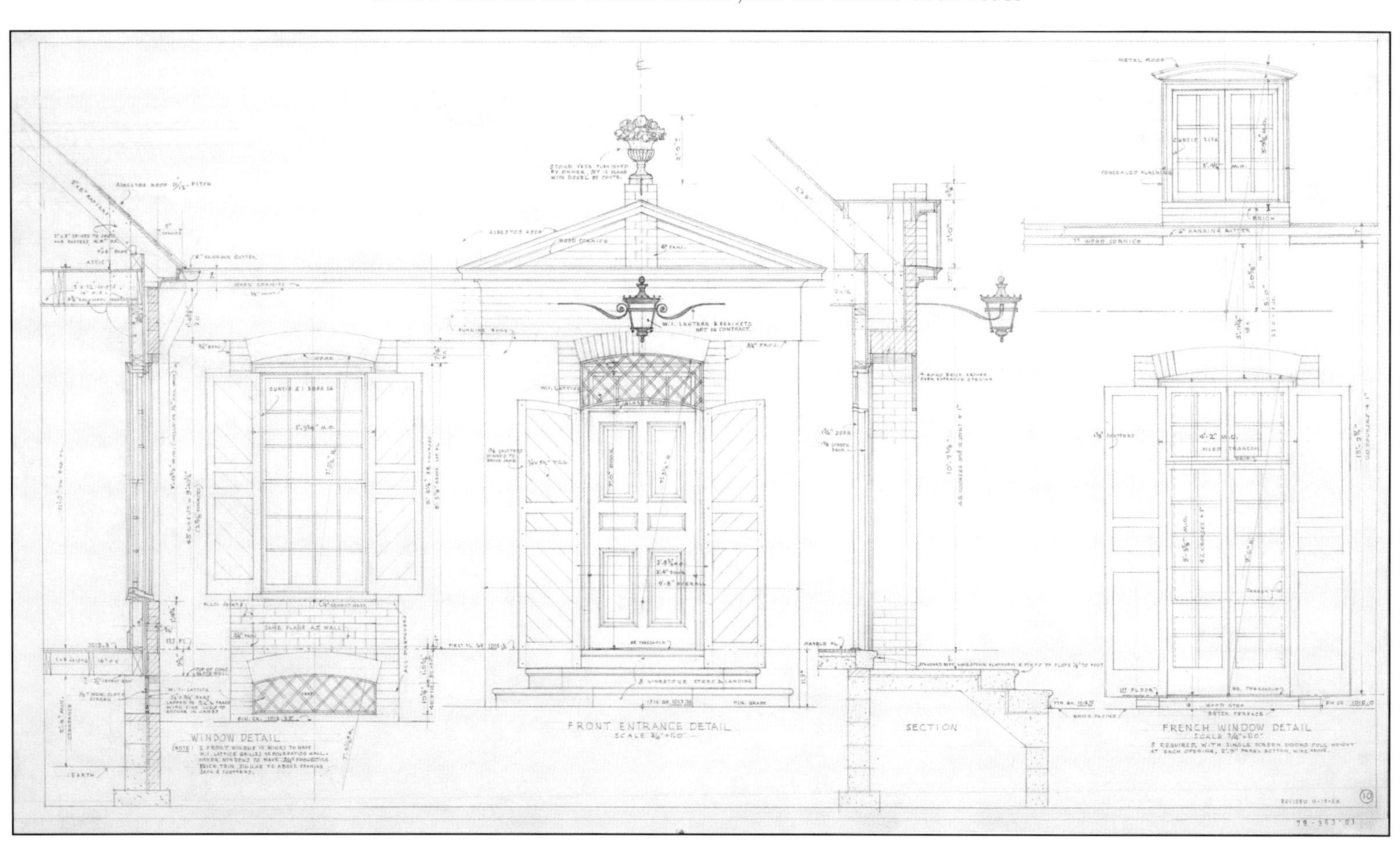

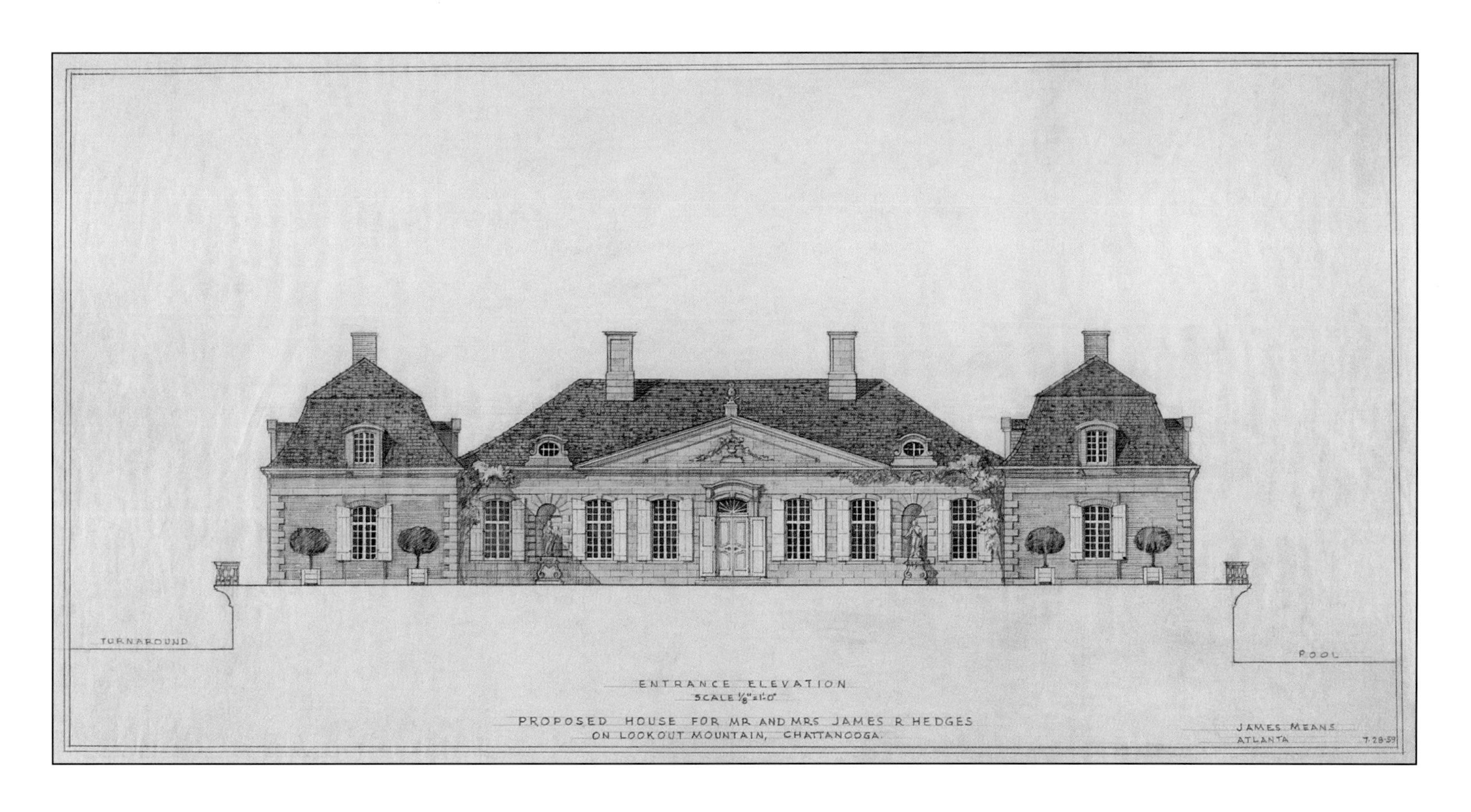

SHADED AND TINTED ELEVATIONS
Above: The proposed elevation for Mr. and Mrs. James R. Hedges (page 46) was modified before construction.
Below: This handsome rendering was for the Dickey house at Stone Mountain Plantation, near Atlanta.

Selected Works

Although James Means's architectural career spanned almost sixty years, from 1917 until early 1979, in which he was involved with the design and construction of a great variety of types of buildings, during the years from 1954 until his death, he was a residential designer: thirty-four of some fifty-five houses are discussed in this section. (The Chronology and the Portfolio contain certain projects not included in the same depth as here.) The two years of his partnership with Edward Vason Jones of Albany, Georgia, had been also, but not entirely, concentrated on house design and construction. The first house that he did alone in Atlanta, after he returned from Albany, was for a Jones & Means client, Arthur L. Montgomery of Atlanta. There is a Jones & Means rendering for the garden façade of that project. (See page 27.) When the partnership was dissolved, their termination agreement was for Means to take all commissions from Macon north, and Montgomery had been solely a Means contact from his Hentz, Adler & Shutze period.

The French-style Montgomery house is the first of the selected works. They are arranged by completion date in chronological order instead of by design date. In *The Houses of James Means* (1979), the houses were arranged in groups, chronologically, "according to their most obvious style." Here they are strictly chronological, documenting his career year by year and showing from the outset his style versatility, his mastery of the eclecticism of style. That term, eclecticism, was a term much in fashion among architectural historians in the late 1960s and '70s, when scholars, architects, and ordinary folks were beginning to reassess the value of what Mary Catherine Means has called, in her fine introduction to the first book on her father, "the undercurrent of classicism in twentieth century architecture." (See 1979 introduction, Appendix I.)

Represented in color are two Means projects from 1958. One is French in style, and one is American; neither of these is still in the hands of the original client-owner. One from 1959, American, has only a second owner. A 1961 French house, at this writing, belongs to a second owner. In 1963 there are three houses, two American and one European; two of these have the original owners and one, the latter, was not included in the 1979 book and now belongs to a new owner. In 1964 there are six; one of them in the Conclusion is an American farmhouse, currently with its second owner. Four others that year are American, and one is French; only two of these still belong to Means clients, but two owners are close relatives, and only one is new. For 1965, among the selected works, an American project is still the property of the original client. The year 1966 is represented by three houses, all of which are still the homes of those who had them built. All three are American in character; one is the restoration of an old house moved to the property. He had none in 1967, but two, both American, are included from the following year. In 1969 a project that had taken ten years to complete is American. The next year brings another historic-American-style house, which has only had one new owner since it was built. For 1971 one work, American in style, is featured. In 1972 there are four houses, three of which are American, with one project consisting of the restoration of two farmhouses for a family in middle Georgia. One of these, actually completed in 1973, was not published in 1979. The year 1974 has an interesting mixture of three: two French manors and one Italian villa, his only example. One in 1975 is American. Those in the next two years, 1976 and 1977, are also American. Then, in 1978, his last completed project is a Georgia farmhouse re-created entirely of antique materials. At his death, his very last house was unfinished; as completed, it is to be found in the Conclusion.

What is a Jimmy Means house, whatever style was chosen? First, Means continued the early-twentieth-century American country estate tradition, usually with smaller houses on smaller suburban plots, but with the same conviction, attention to detail, and essentially formal planning. The simple life of the agrarian past was idealized but always with a sense of the English country house, or a French *manoir*, or the home of eighteenth-century American colonial gentry in the background. The house was a component of a garden landscape, usually with some outbuildings completing the picture of genteel country life. The entire movement was, in fact, often called "house and garden." (In 1901 the shelter magazine by that name was founded by a group of Philadelphia architects led by Wilson Eyre, Jr.)

A house should fit its site, seeming to have been there as a homeplace for a long time. It should fit appropriately into its landscape and region. A gamut of period styles were used as models, which were subtly transformed. These included Southern plantation idioms, and sometimes the regional interpretations were quite imaginative, for example, Mediterranean styles transposed to Florida because of its Spanish colonial history.

The goal was not what might be called scientific history, but instead creative eclecticism, a term coined in the early 1960s for extending styles within their original spirit for a fundamentally classic approach, with authentic floor plans, details, material, and crafts. In the 1980s, the phrases "classical language of architecture" and "style vocabulary" were much discussed at symposia. Callie Huger Efird expressed it this way in her editorial notes for her 1979 Means book: "[Whatever the style] the details and proportions of a Means house 'ruined' a client for anything else. Spacious dimensions, symmetry, repetition of shapes, bold molding, detailed chimney breast, high ceilings—there are only a few of his design preferences." With reference to overall plans, she wrote, "He often used a T-shape, mainly to gain double light exposure for as many rooms as possible. [Her own Means house had this plan.] Quite a few two-story houses were built on the old wide hall, four on four plan." (The T-shape was a historic Southern house plan, sometimes used in modified form by members of the Georgia school of classicists; for his own home in Atlanta Lewis Edmund Crook Jr. effectively merged the Southern dogtrot plan and the T-shape. Like "Buck" Crook, Means knew first hand vernacular classicism and how to adapt it in this own designs.)

The American colonial revival was clearly part of the house and garden movement. Following World War I, the era in which Means's architectural consciousness (and conscience) was molded, early American art, architecture, and decorative arts became practically a religion. In 1924, the American Wing of the Metropolitan Museum of Art opened, and soon thereafter Colonial Williamsburg was conceived and incorporated. House and garden pilgrimages, especially in the South, were popular. (This writer's first was at Charleston, South Carolina, in 1958.)

People sought the security of deep-seated tradition, or at least what was perceived in those terms. France had been a ally during the Revolution and the Great War, so French styles were always suitable and considered stylish, as was any sort of Italianate; the villa was a house and garden ideal, and Palladio was the reigning genius of the continuing revival of Renaissance classicism. The educated and well-to-do, and those who aspired to be, were the clients. Together, architect and client and their friends and acquaintances became coteries, originally, of course, a French artistic concept describing a close circle of devotees.

One Means client once told this writer that she had belonged to a "brotherhood" when Jimmy Means was building her house. Definitely that is what Means clients became, together searching for and exchanging old, seasoned building materials and information about old houses, sites, and furnishings, looking for ideas and for old outbuildings and old plants, as well as, possible building sites for themselves or others. Means often traveled with them. Dr. and Mrs. Herbert West say that Means "traveled light, only with a toothbrush."

A Jimmy Means house began with a vision, then a piece of land, not of property, but land, soil, with a creek or river, if at all possible, and trees. The placement of the house on the land according to his landscape scheme was vital and a forte of Means's.

For this book, the James Lockhart photography has quite consciously been crafted to show the house in relation to its setting, the land, gardens, trees. The client was lucky to get a garage, if it all, for this was a coterie that preferred, at least in theory, barns and stables to garages, horses to horseless carriages. The same applied to bathrooms, kitchens, and closets. They, especially the architect, would really have preferred outbuildings for storage and other necessities, such as cooking.

This was a suburban gentry. One Means house, shown in the Conclusion, was two blocks from an expressway (I-75) in what had once been rolling farmland in northwest Fulton County, Georgia. The pre-expressway past was more convenient, however, with a superhighway, a supermarket, and a service station nearby.

These homes were considered appropriate for modern living, a restful, comfortable, familiar background for a world compromised by nuclear power and bombs; the future, yes, but with a secure sense of enduring history, a sense of place—homeplace—that these selected James Means houses were, are, and (with love and luck) will have. They are part of the legacy of that "Maverick from Meansville," Georgia, "Saint Jimmy," and his client friends and new generations of admiring homeowners. One of these, a Means client, Virginia Shapard (page 108), summed it up aptly for the 1979 house book: "The scale, proportion, detail of design and millwork, grace and symmetry of our home are a product of the genius of James Means, who enjoyed watching the building grow over a protracted period of time and shared with the owners their joy, pride of work and participation in the project."

In the following Selected Works, if a house has two names, the first is that of the original Means client, and the second is the owner/resident at the time of this account. The historic style given, as in the 1979 Means book, is based on the most salient characteristics of the entrance façade. The Means design vocabulary, his eye for scale, proportion, and historic detail, was subtle and well-studied. Principles of classic design were more important for Means than the obvious style chosen. He was not a copyist, but a learned eclectic with finesse, understanding the essential elements of the beauty of various precedents for present needs and pleasure. The page numbers for The Houses of James Means *apply to the 1979 first edition and the 1985 reprint with revisions.*

MONTGOMERY-PORTMAN HOUSE

Means client: Arthur L. Montgomery and Eleanor Morgan Montgomery.
Place: Atlanta. Completion Date: October 1956; second floor of garage, 1971.
Current Owner: Mr. and Mrs. John C. Portman III.
Style: Provincial French.
Contractor/builder: Barge and Co.
Millwork: Jesse Jones, Cornelia, Georgia.
Later architect: John C. Portman III.
Interim Owners: Stephen P. Fricano, Dr. and Mrs. John C. Rieser.
The Houses of James Means, *pp. 76–77.*

This French-provincial-style manor house is a Means masterpiece. Trained in the eighteenth-century way by apprenticeship to master designers in the Georgia school of classicists, Means produced this house in the original sense of the word masterpiece, for it was his first major commission entirely on his own. It is certainly worthy of such a highly complimentary designation. As with all his designs, Means personally supervised every aspect—selecting seasoned building materials from demolished old buildings—so that the finished house, inside and out, was perfectly handcrafted, seeming from the first like an "old house."

Looking as though it had been

Left: Front entrance elevation.
Above: Front entrance details.

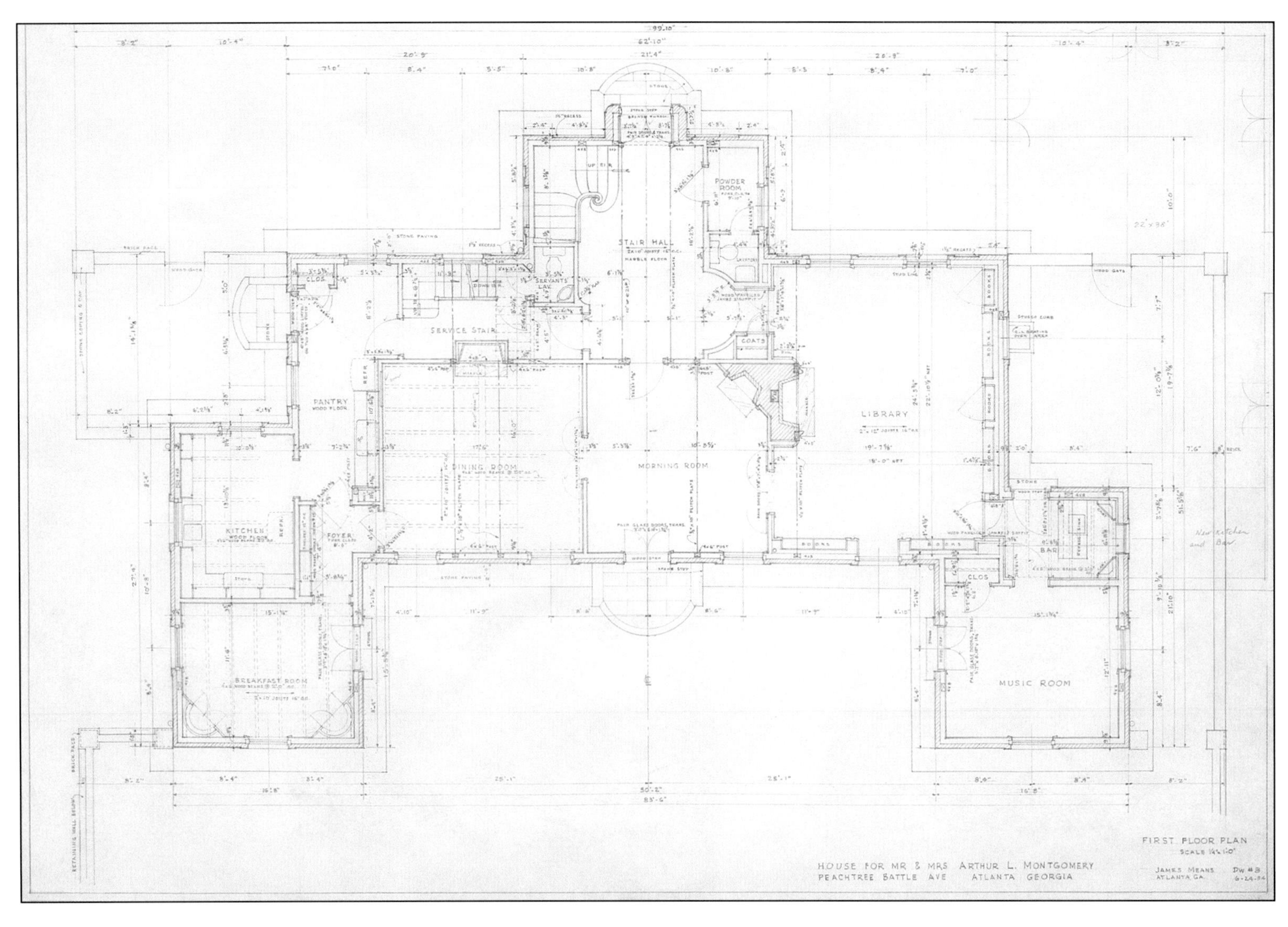

MONTGOMERY-PORTMAN HOUSE. First floor plan.

placed on this romantic ridge during the reign of Louis XV (c. 1750), in fact, it was completed in 1956 as the home of Arthur L. Montgomery and his family. Means based his design on the mid-eighteenth-century Girard house at Vézelay, a hill town in Burgundy. The Montgomerys, wanting a French house, visited and photographed the Girard house.

Means owned a copy of *The Tuileries Brochures*, published in 1932 by the Ludowici-Celadon Company, makers of Ludowici tile. Containing many photographs of the tile-roofed Girard house, with its dormers placed at the eaves in the French style, the article comments about small French houses, in villages, that recognize a fundamental principle of scale: "a small thing must have fewer parts and motifs than a large one." That well summarizes the character of Means's domestic architecture, whatever style he and his clients chose.

The style of Louis XV is known for its comfortable domestic scale, especially as interpreted in the provinces. A reaction against the grandeur of Louis XIV, this style was a forerunner of the best of eclectic twentieth-century residential design. (David Adler, 1882–1949, of Chicago, built several fine adaptations of this style in the Chicago suburbs just prior to World War I.)

James Means captured the appeal of the original French provincial prototypes. With mansard roof and arched dormer windows, it is a symmetrical, pleasantly formal house of grey stucco over bricks, entered from a motor forecourt on the north elevation through a boxwood garden parterre. Around the central axis of a main stair hall, as is the custom in this style, are distributed rooms for specific functions: a paneled library, a morning, a dining, a music, and a breakfast room. Generous French windows and doors take advantage of vistas of the wooded terrain. Peachtree Creek, eighty feet below the south terrace elevation, is a beautiful natural landscape feature as it flows toward the site of one of the old Howell mills. The rural illusion, similar to that of the house at Vézelay, is what Means and his clients sought, but the lights of downtown Atlanta skyscrapers are only a few miles to the south.

This house yearly confirms the style of Louis XV as an appropriate one for our own day. The latest owner, John C. Portman III, himself an architect (but a modernist), and his wife Erin, love their Jimmy Means house and are carefully renovating it as a home for their young family.

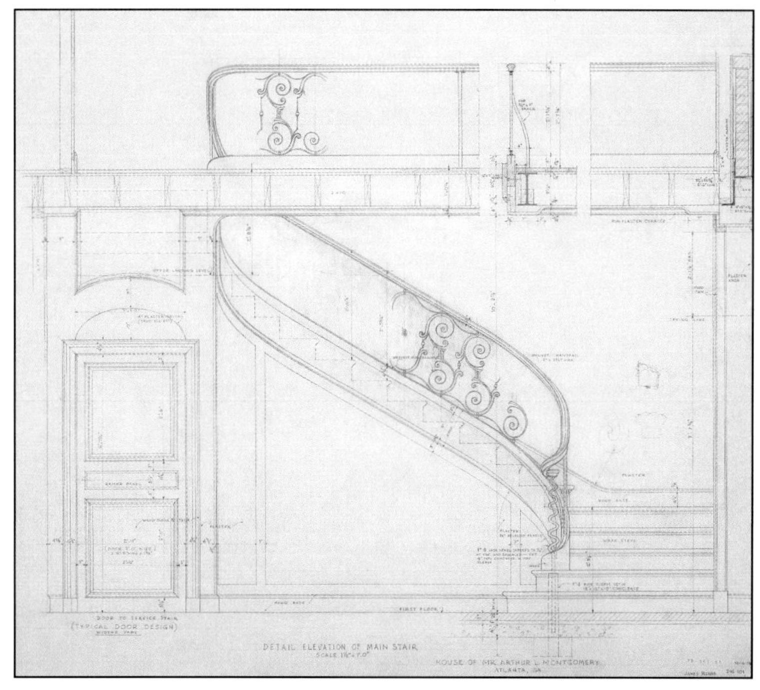

Montgomery-Portman House.
Top left: Detail elevation of main stair. Top right: Stair hall.
Left: Morning room. Above: Stair hall detail.

COOK-VAWTER HOUSE

Means client: Mr. and Mrs. Marcus A. Cook, Jr.
Place: Atlanta. Completion Date: January 1958.
Current Owner: Mr. and Mrs. Wesley R. Vawter III.
Style: Provincial French.
Contractor/builder: Wesley Moran.
Interim Owners: Mr. and Mrs. Cleveland Willcoxon (1970), Mr. and Mrs. Lindsey Hopkins III.
The Houses of James Means, *pp. 78–79.*

During the summer of 1999 this became the Cook-Vawter house, when Mr. and Mrs. Wesley R. (Terry) Vawter III purchased it as their home from Mr. and Mrs. Lindsey Hopkins III. There have been several owners since the Marcus Cooks, and each has added livable aspects, the Cleveland Wilcoxon's swimming pool, for example, but Means's French vernacular architecture is the main attraction of this beautifully sited and landscaped residence on the highest hill in the Kingswood neighborhood of Buckhead, just off Atlanta's West Paces Ferry Road. Its tall chimney stacks announce that this is an old-fashioned house, with working fireplaces, probably with fine French mantelpieces, all of which has been the simple truth for each of the owners of this elegantly simple Jimmy Means house.

As with Means's other French houses, he achieved his design goals with an economy of elements, suggesting modestly, in a gentlemanly voice, the style precedents he was emulating. The carved limestone urn on a brick plinth above the bold, pedimented classic frontispiece of the projecting entrance is the sole bit of "French fuss," except for the wrought-iron lantern lighting the doorway, worthy of a fashionable

Opposite: Entrance elevation.
Above: Entrance detail.

Parisian side street, and casting shadows through the iron latticework transom. The limestone trim, the high-pitched roofs, the balanced pavilion wings, the solid paneled shutters, and the shuttered entrance all suggest the style with just the right measure of grace notes—"nothing too much"—all perfectly suited to the symmetrical mass of the house. The plan, featuring a wide transverse entrance hall paved in a bold pattern of black-and-white marble, testifies to Means's mastery of the livable period house, not overly embellished with Frenchness, inside or out, but just enough understated good taste to charm every fortunate passerby and favored visitor.

As is characteristic of the eighteenth-century prototypes for this classic domestic style, the classical orders are not used but are suggested by the orderliness of the composition and by some of the interior and exterior moldings. Comparison with the Montgomery-Portman house, which preceded the Cook-Vawter house by several years, shows that Means was capable of variety and fresh solutions within the traditional framework of eighteenth-century French provincial classicism.

The current owner, Wesley Vawter, knows the enduring market value of a Jimmy Means house. Vawter is a successful real estate agent specializing in northside Atlanta houses. A founding board member of Southern Architecture Foundation Inc., he was in his mid fifties when he purchased his Means house, Means's age when he completed it for the Marcus Cooks in 1958.

Cook-Vawter House.
Opposite top: Entrance hall.
Opposite bottom: Stair hall.
Above: Dining room.
Right: Living room.

PLOWDEN-DUNAWAY HOUSE

Means client: Mr. and Mrs. Will Best Plowden.
Place: Griffin, Georgia. Completion Date: May 1958.
Current Owner: Dr. and Mrs. James B. Dunaway.
Style: American Georgian colonial.
Contractor/builder: Barge & Co., Atlanta.
Millwork: O'Neill, Rome, Georgia.
The Houses of James Means, *pp. 28–29.*

Opposite: Entrance portico. Above: Rear elevation.

The colonial revival in America, which started before the turn of the century, came to fruition and maturity in the 1920s and 1930s with the creation of Colonial Williamsburg, Inc., in Virginia. The plans for the Will Best Plowden house are dated 1957, almost seventeen years after its inspiration, the George Wythe house, was restored in 1939 at Williamsburg. Built circa 1753, the two-story brick Wythe mansion is often considered the handsomest house in the restoration village. (*See* Means's diagrammatic study of the proportional system for a Virginia house similar to the Wythe House, page 9.)

Anne Hightower Plowden and Will Plowden moved into their home, with three children, in May 1958. Mr. Plowden commented in *The Houses of James Means*, "Jimmy Means went to Williamsburg with us. We tried to obtain the plans for the Wythe House, but were not allowed to use them. We purchased 50 photographs made during the restoration that were very helpful. Jimmy counted brick courses, measured moldings, sketched interiors, making notes about details. We wanted to be as authentic as possible. The front portico is a copy of one on the Randolph-Semple House." (The design of that post-colonial house, c. 1782, also in Williamsburg, has been attributed to Thomas Jefferson.)

Anne Hightower Plowden was quite familiar with the colonial revival and with James Means, because her parents, Julian and Grace Hightower of Thomaston, Georgia, built in 1947–49 an adaptation of James Madison's Montpelier, designed by Philip Shutze, assisted by James Means. In 1962 the Hightowers enclosed an open porch there, and Grace Hightower told this writer in 1981 that she believed Means had played a crucial part in the creation of their house and of the porch enclosure. That the Plowdens chose Means to design their home on stately old East College Street in Griffin, Georgia, seems quite natural.

The central block of the Plowden house, based on the Wythe House

down to brick courses, has wings to provide a kitchen, guest room, and dressing room, functional elements for which, it has sometimes been said, Means had little use. Seldom, if ever, was it his priority. (Means told one client, "Get rid of some of your clothes, and we can make smaller closets and dressing rooms.)

After the death of both the Plowdens, and after admiring this house for years, Dr. and Mrs. James Dunaway purchased the Plowden house in 1996 to be a homeplace in which to raise their own family. Their love of the place is so genuine and joyous that they seem to have been Means's clients. Clearly this is a Means house in highly appreciative hands. (See preface for the author's firsthand knowledge of this house, as it was being completed in 1958.)

Two other interesting connections between the architect and his Plowden clients provide a glimpse of a South, now almost gone, in which the Georgia classicist lived and practiced. James Means and Anne Hightower Plowden were almost blood kin, cousins. The first wife of Means's father, John Francis Means, was Ella Eugenia Hightower, whom he married in 1878. She was Captain William (Billy) Hightower's daughter and an aunt of Julian Hightower, Anne Hightower's father. Ella Means, who died in 1882, is buried with three Means babies in the Hightower plot in the old Glenwood Cemetery at Thomaston, Georgia. These are Jimmy Means's half-siblings. The second connection is that Will Best Plowden's family was from Dickey, Georgia (west of Albany). The antebellum Plowden house from there is the neoclassical main house at the Stone Mountain Plantation project. Means had moved and renovated the house in the early 1960s. (See page 27.)

Plowden-Dunaway House.
Right: Sitting room.
Above: Breakfast room.

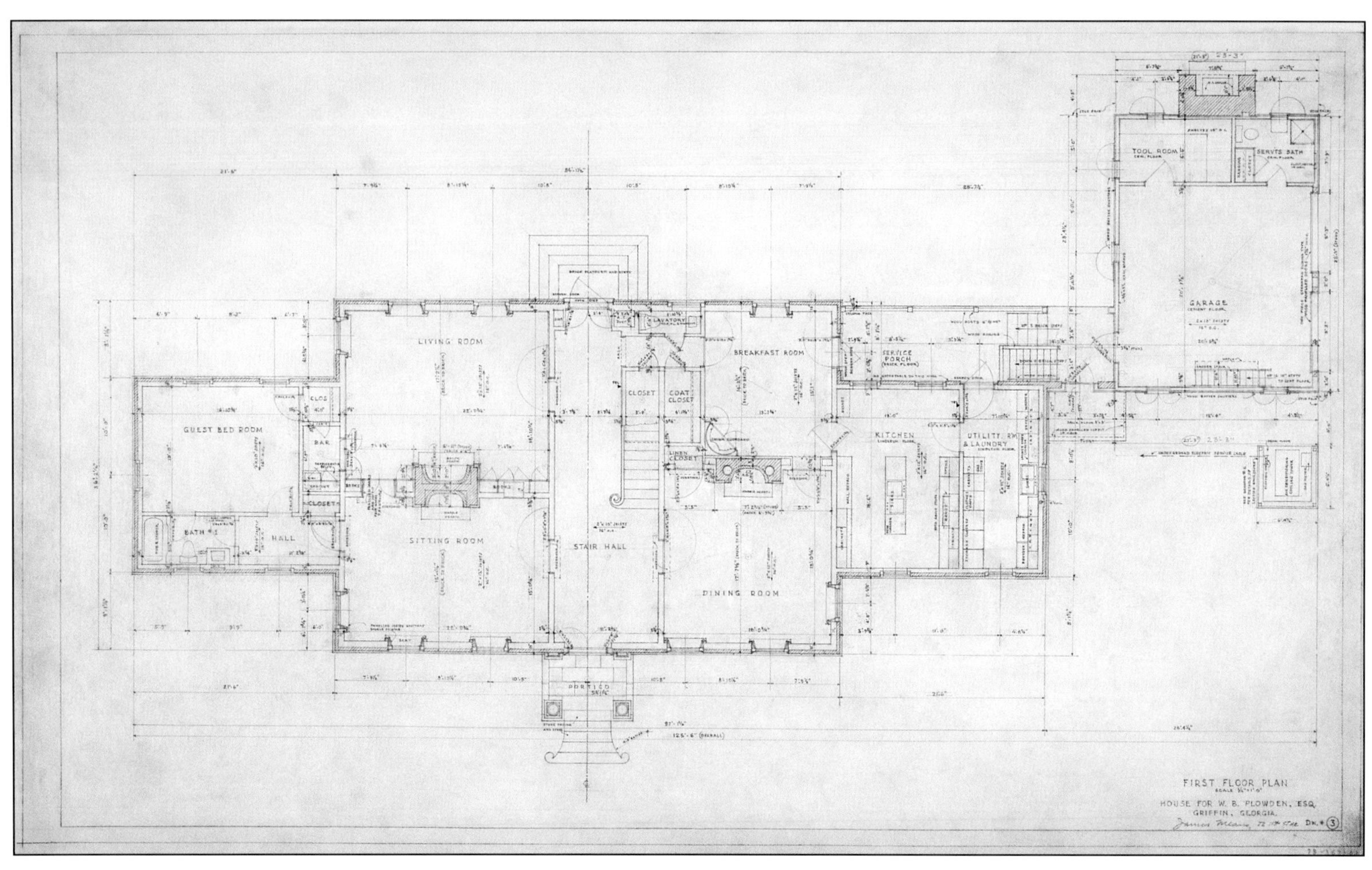
LIVING ROOM
BREAKFAST ROOM
SERVICE PORCH
GUEST BED ROOM
CLOS
BAR
CLOSET
COAT CLOSET
LINEN CLOSET
KITCHEN
UTILITY RM & LAUNDRY
TOOL ROOM
SERV'TS BATH
GARAGE
BATH #1
HALL
SITTING ROOM
STAIR HALL
DINING ROOM
PORTICO
FIRST FLOOR PLAN
HOUSE FOR W. B. PLOWDEN, ESQ.
GRIFFIN, GEORGIA.
Dw. # 3

Plowden-Dunaway House.
Opposite top: Dining room. Opposite bottom: First floor plan. Above: Living room.

BLOOM-WILLINGHAM HOUSE

Means client: Dr. and Mrs. Walter L. Bloom.
Place: Cobb County, Georgia. Completion Date: 1959.
Current Owner: Mr. and Mrs. Thomas M. Willingham.
Style: Early-eighteenth-century colonial, Maryland eastern shore.
Contractor/builder: Dan Brothers.
Millwork: Jim Girdler, W. P. Stephens Lumber Co.
The Houses of James Means, *pp. 12–13.*

When Dr. and Mrs. Walter Lyon Bloom became Means clients in the late 1950s, there were sixty-five acres in this tract along the Cobb County, Georgia, side of the Chattahoochee River; the area was semi-rural, and the acreage was enough to count as a farm. Means and the Blooms built a house reminiscent of the early-eighteenth-century farmhouses of the eastern shore of Maryland. The most characteristic early Maryland aspect of their Chattahoochee country house is its picturesque gambrel roof. This gable with a double slope came to the Chesapeake from England in the seventeenth century. Sometimes called in the South a Dutch roof, it is a charming way of enlarging attic headroom.

The Blooms had moved to east Cobb County before it became part of the suburban sprawl of Atlanta, as it did in the 1970s and 1980s. Even so, in 1977, when Mr. and Mrs. Thomas M. Willingham bought the place from the Blooms, the house still had enough tree-screened privacy on its high hill above the river and the bottom pastureland below to suit their needs exactly. The Willinghams were able to acquire eight acres of the original tract. In fact, they helped save the house from becoming a clubhouse for a development. A relative who knew about the place and Jimmy Means's exceptional architecture encouraged them; they have never regretted their decision.

In 1959 the Blooms believed they had built a house with the aura of the period of its early American architecture style. Today that sense of old time and place is even more persistent. The perfection of the antique red brick, which is laid in the Flemish bond pattern favored in the South in the colonial period, has forty more years of patina. Now the surprise of finding Means's design, up the winding driveway off now-busy Johnson Ferry Road, is even more pronounced.

Because the area has grown from semirural quiet to a bustling fast-food suburbia, the authenticity and uncanny craft excellence of Means's practically unadorned Maryland plantation architectural style stands out even more than before. It provides the Willinghams and their visitors a visual respite from the multitudes of instant "traditional homes" that have mushroomed in recent years throughout that area. Means's understated colonial re-creation has become a classic landmark worth preserving, from an era that has passed, even if from less than fifty years ago.

Opposite page: Entrance elevation.
Left: Entrance garden.
Below: Stair hall.
Bottom: Living room.

HEDGES-SIMMONS HOUSE

Means client: Mrs. James R. Hedges.
Place: Lookout Mountain, Georgia. Completion Date: February 1961.
Current Owner: Mr. and Mrs. Mitchell F. Simmons.
Style: Provincial French.
Contractor/builder: Winston Bland, Chattanooga.
Millwork: Jesse L. Jones, Cornelia, Georgia.
The Houses of James Means, *pp. 80–81.*

Above: Entrance elevation and courtyard.
Opposite top: Living room.
Opposite bottom: Elevations of paneled walls in living room.

Almost twenty years after its completion, the home of Mrs. James R. (Dot) Hedges was the lead feature of the 1980 winter issue of *Southern Accents* magazine; the article was entitled "Le Petit Chantecaille, a French Chateau on Lookout Mountain." The cover pictured the Italian marble-floored foyer with balancing niches covered with hard-blocked Dufour wallpaper, still in place today.

Dramatic photographs captured Mrs. Hedges's elegant perch on Chattanooga's Lookout Mountain, overlooking the valley below and the mountains beyond. Credits included James Means's French architecture and the French interior design by two knowledgeable stalwarts from Atlanta's W.E. Browne Decorating Company, David Byers and Charles Townsend. The article mentioned the recently published *Houses of James Means*, "commemorating the works of the late architect." (Today Mrs. Hedges and all the other talented people mentioned, as well as the Atlanta decorating firm, are no more.) During the year following this splendid piece, the house went on the market.

The purchasers were Mitchell and Frances Hames Simmons, the proud and well-satisfied current owners, who preserve the spirit of the home that James Means and the late Dot Hedges designed and built over forty years ago. The Simmonses first moved to Lookout Mountain a few years before the Hedges house was completed; they have long recognized the mountain suburb's exceptional quality and beauty.

Mrs. Hedges was the sort of locally celebrated lady who was often called a grande dame, as she was in the 1980 magazine article. This French term is appropriate, because Mrs. Hedges was a Francophile whose grandfather had been a French military hero under Napoleon III. A recognized admirer of French decorative arts, she called on Browne Decorating Company to help find antique mantelpieces and paneling

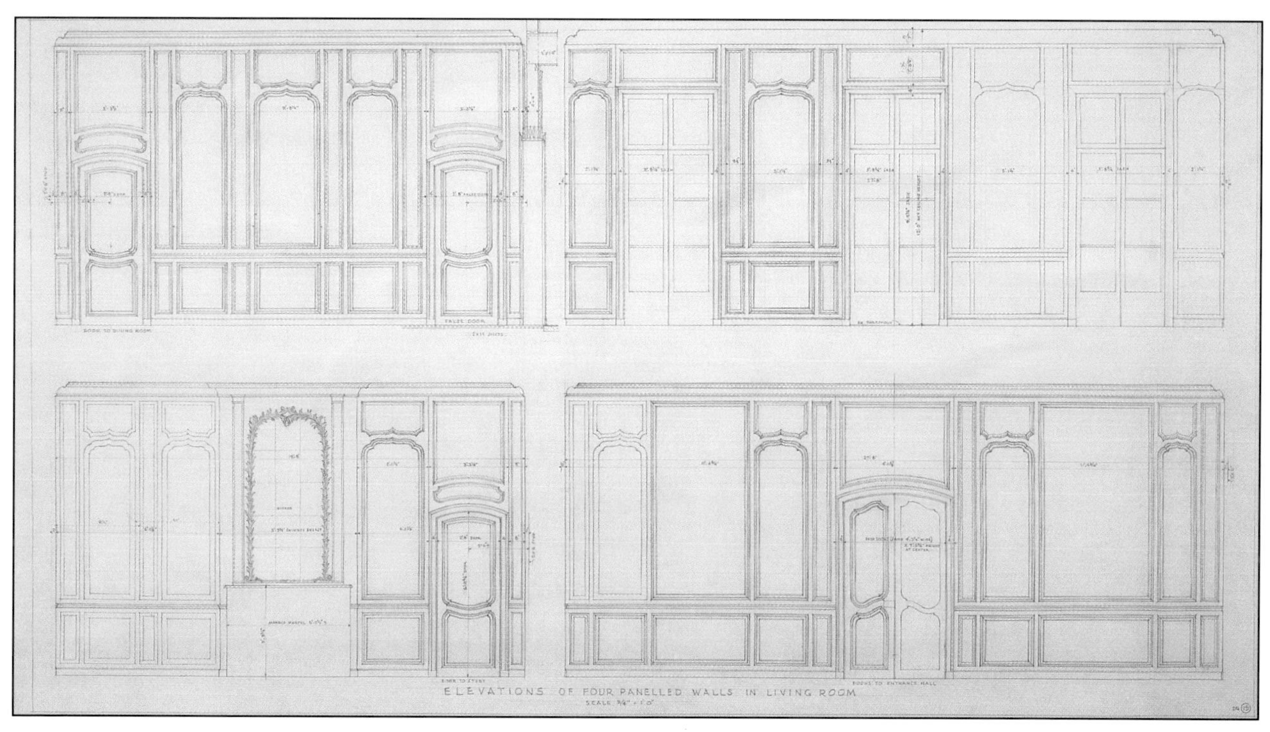
DOORS TO ENTRANCE HALL
ELEVATIONS OF FOUR PANELLED WALLS IN LIVING ROOM

HEDGES-SIMMONS HOUSE. Above: Entrance hall with view into living room and stair hall. Below: Stair hall from entrance hall. Opposite top: Dining room. Opposite bottom: First floor plan.

for her home.

This was the third French house that Means designed; he again used his 1931–32 *The Tuileries Brochures: With Special Reference to Roofs of Tile*, as he had for Arthur Montgomery in Atlanta. The Chateau of Chantecaille at Touraine, a southern district of France, was well illustrated in the brochure in several places. Like "Le petit Chantecaille," it is also sited on the edge of a valley. Begun in the fifteenth century, it was enlarged in the period of Louis XIV when dormers were added outside and paneled woodwork, inside. It sat in a formal *jardin a la Francaise*. Means did not copy the chateau, which was called in the brochure "an ensemble of great majesty

due to its calm, its honesty, and its absolute correctness." As Mrs. Hedges wrote for *The Houses of James Means*, "Mr. Means did a marvelous job of reproducing the feel of the place."

Means's front elevation rendering on page 27 is a more ambitious façade than was actually built, but the two are close cousins. Three eave-line dormers on the main block, a large central one and two balancing *"oeil-de-boeuf"* windows, all three similar to those on the French model, grace this mountaintop chateau. The Simmonses adore their classic Means creation, much as had the late *"chatelaine,"* Dot Hedges, of Chattanooga's Le petit Chantecaille. (Chantecaille refers to singing quail.)

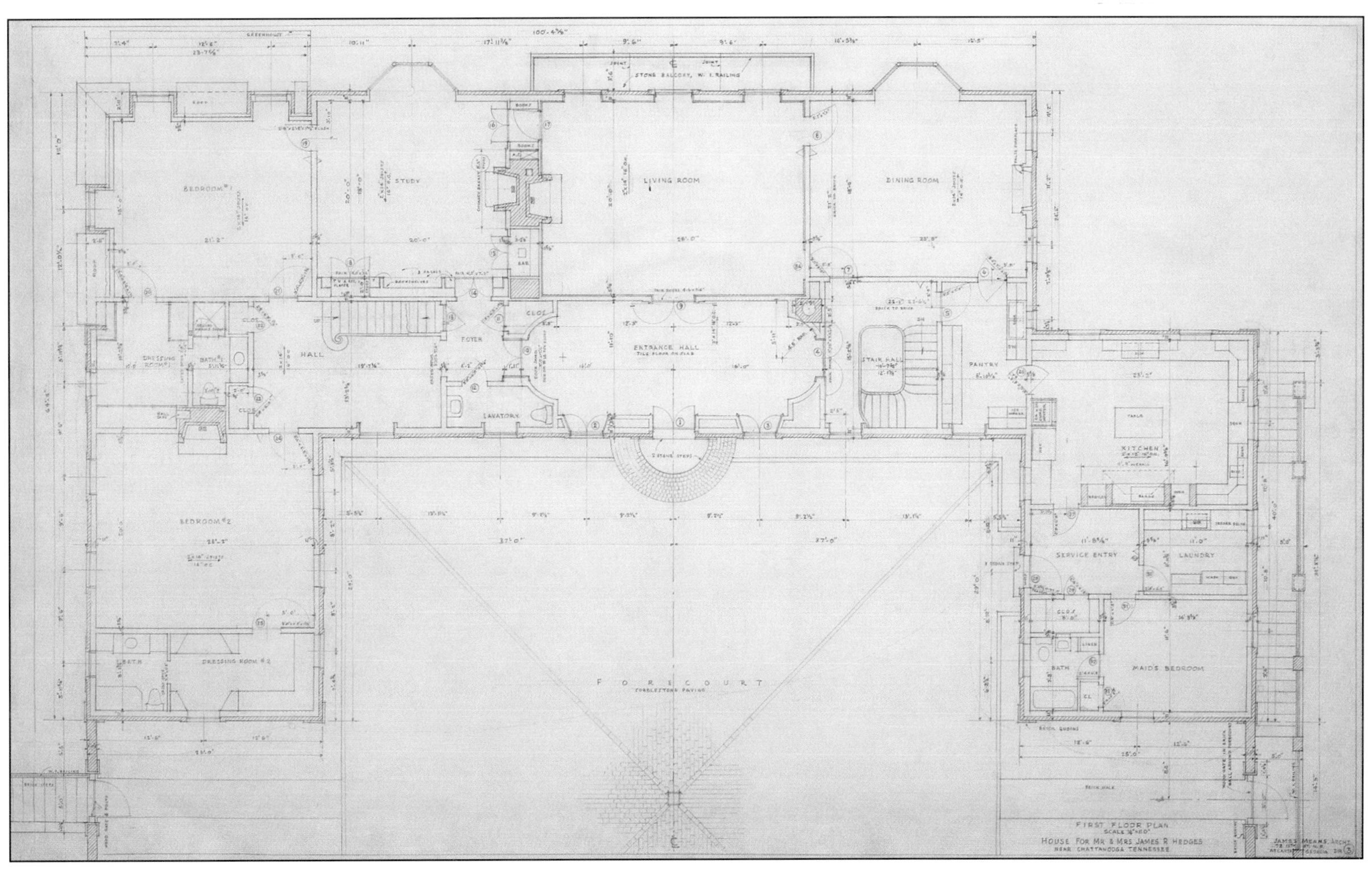
STONE BALCONY, W. I. RAILING
BEDROOM #1
STUDY
LIVING ROOM
DINING ROOM
HALL
FOYER
ENTRANCE HALL
TILE FLOOR ON SLAB
STAIR HALL
PANTRY
LAVATORY
DRESSING ROOM #1
BATH #1
CLOS.
BAR
2 STONE STEPS
KITCHEN
SERVICE ENTRY
LAUNDRY
MAIDS BEDROOM
BATH
BEDROOM #2
DRESSING ROOM #2
FORECOURT
BRICK WALK
FIRST FLOOR PLAN
HOUSE FOR MR & MRS JAMES R HEDGES
NEAR CHATTANOOGA TENNESSEE

DENDER HOUSE

Means client: Judge and Mrs. William Madison Dender.
Place: Etowah, Tennessee. Completion Date: Fall, 1963.
Style: Southern neoclassical.
Contractor/builder: owner.
Millwork: Jesse Jones, Cornelia, Georgia.
The Houses of James Means, *pp. 48–49.*

Andever is the name Judge William and Nancy Dender gave their home. "And ever" is certainly appropriate. They built it with James Means; they have been here ever since. If ever there was a modern homeplace, Andever is it, forever and a day. This is indeed home for them and the five sons they reared here.

Natives of Etowah, Tennessee, the Denders had located 127 acres of land outside that town before they met Means. They even owned a Neel Reid spiral staircase from the J. Carroll Payne house (on Peachtree Street near Brookwood train station), which they saw in place before the Payne house was demolished in 1959. The day they bought it,

Top: Entrance elevation. Above: Rear elevation. Opposite: Drawing of entrance portico details.

antique dealer Kenneth Garcia, Sr., was also on the site, and he encouraged them to buy it and some other materials. Later they found a carpenter back home in Etowah, Otis Moses, who said, "I know how that staircase goes together." They also acquired from the Payne house a Palladian window, bay window, and curved door.

Garcia, a friend and associate of Jimmy Means, encouraged them also to use Means eventually as their architect. James Means, Nancy Dender says, "Stuck us in his car and took us to all the houses he was building." The Denders had been collecting old materials on their own to use in building their home. "We met Jimmy Means at the Hedges house [then under construction] at Chattanooga the first time." "We had visited architect Philip Shutze at his Candler Building office, and he suggested we see Jimmy Means; that was in 1961." The Denders "talked with Jimmy about two years before he did any drawings." Nancy had a "box full of ideas." They went to see Means's work at the Stone Mountain Plantation complex near Atlanta, where he was restoring some seventeen buildings he had helped locate for the restoration project.

Judge Dender had actually thought he wanted to build a Frank Lloyd

Wright sort of house. But that was before they got to know and travel with the Georgia classicist, Jimmy Means. Together he and Means and Nancy made a Southern neoclassical house, federal style in some details, Greek revival in others, altogether reminiscent of houses built by carpenter-architects with their owners throughout the antebellum South. The rear is reminiscent of Shadows-on-the-Teche in New Iberia, Louisiana. Most of the building materials, including the fluted Doric columns, six in all, are old; the Denders collected these materials for seven years.

Means helped them site the house on a slight elevation at the end of a long drive, through farmland, leading straight to the house. It was Means's favorite driveway pattern. Formal gardens lie to the north and south. All in all, Andever is a perfect legacy of the James Means phenomenon, where client and architect were a friendly team; they were made for each other, and what they fashioned is a "beaut," to use old American slang appropriate for this very Southern-American house.

Dender House.
Opposite top: Stair hall.
Opposite bottom: Living room.

Above: Rear gallery.
Left: View from hall into dining room.

HAVERTY HOUSE

Means client: Mr. and Mrs. Rawson Haverty, Sr.
Place: Atlanta. Completion Date: October 1963.
Style: Southern colonial Georgian.
Contractor/builder: Vann H. Beane.
Millwork: Jim Girdler, W. P. Stephens Co., Marietta.
The Houses of James Means, *pp. 30–31.*

Left: Entrance elevation and motor court.
Above: Rear elevation.

In his *Ain't The Roses Sweet* (1989), Rawson Haverty Sr. has an extraordinary personal account of the creation of his and Margaret Munnerlyn Haverty's Atlanta home, into which they moved in the late summer of 1963 before it was quite finished; the painter "for a time became a regular part of our family," Rawson wrote.

These excerpts tell the story in the client's own enlightening words: "We purchased from Bates Block a piece of land at the end of Paces Valley Road. It consisted of 7 1/2 acres at the intersection of Wolf and Nancy Creeks. An acre or so was flood land with a red barn, and there was an acre or so of lovely hilltop. I loved it; Margaret thought it was too far out, but she got her friend Jimmy Means to begin drawing plans for a Georgian-style house, which is what she wanted."

Mr. Haverty continued: "Margaret and Jimmy Means went to work on the house plans. He did a half-dozen sketches, all classics, and as he learned about our budget he cut back and cut back. Finally he produced a set of plans which he hoped we could afford. I asked my friend Alvin Barge to bid, and the results were too high, so Jimmy suggested that we do it ourselves. He knew a good foreman, Vann Beane, who told us he could build the house for under $100,000. That was the top of our budget. . . . We broke ground in July 1962. Jimmy and Margaret worked together for over a year. I stopped by each morning before work, and each evening after."

Rawson Haverty's firsthand account and his summary could stand for the experience and opinions of numerous other Means clients: "Jimmy Means was unique, and perhaps a genius. He worked alone, no draftsmen, no secretary. He drew every line. He supervised the placement of every board. In the face of our impatience and frustrations, he was unbelievably patient. The process of building was strenuous for everyone, but we hung together, survived and saw it through. The house became a wonderful home, and Jimmy Means went on to build some of the most gracious houses in the South."

The experience of building their home is indelibly etched in the Havertys' memories. Interviews with them

over the course of research for this book also produced the following interesting sidelights. "We found wide heart pine lumber at Athens, Georgia, which was used throughout the house. W. P. Stephens Company broke so many blades on the nails in the old wood that Stephens had to start using a metal detector." Margaret Haverty said that she and Jimmy Means finished the heart-pine floors in the dining room themselves, and Rawson Haverty said that Jimmy helped Margaret wax the Charleston brick floors in the entrance hall.

The Havertys agreed that a tree in the back garden became the anchor for the axis of the entire house. They also love the old brick front with its formal cobblestoned courtyard and entrance piers, at the same time as loving the informality of the frame rear elevation, because it makes the Georgian house seem more Southern. They recalled, "Jimmy swore ours was the last do-it-yourself, cut-corners, project, he would ever do." Lastly, they pointed out the ivory "peace button" ornamenting the top of the staircase newel post in the entrance hall. Rawson said, "We placed it there at a party when peace had been made with the architect, the builder, and the banker."

On the dust jacket of *Ain't The Roses Sweet*, Rawson Haverty, Sr., is pictured at home in the paneled library, stained a warm honey beige; it is a peaceful scene of an Atlanta business, civic, and church leader as he retired as CEO of the Haverty Furniture Company, founded in 1885 by his grandfather.

Haverty House.
Opposite: Entrance/stair hall.
Top: Dining room.
Above: Living room.

SHACKELFORD-CARSPECKEN HOUSE

Means client: Francis and Renee F. Shackelford.
Place: Atlanta. Completion Date: 1963.
Current Owner: Dr. and Mrs. H. Hutson Carspecken.
Style: Italianate villa; 1912, J. Neel Reid.
Later architect: Norman Davenport Askins, 1989.
Not included in The Houses of James Means.

James Means's design for Francis and Renee Shackelford has a special place in his domestic architecture, because it is his homage to his mentor, J. Neel Reid, whose hands he became in the early 1920s when Reid himself could no longer draft. This 1963 design is an expression of Means's maturity as one of the last practicing members of the Georgia school of classicists.

The Shackelford house is Means's creative recasting of one of Neel Reid's early great classic houses, the Hunter Cooper of 1912, an Italianate villa that stood, until it was torn down in the spring of 1963, in the Brookwood neighborhood of Atlanta's Peachtree Road.

Highly regarded locally when it was built, the Cooper house was illustrated nationally in the December 1917 issue of *Architectural Record*. In that issue's Portfolio of Current Architecture, there were two exterior views of it, the entrance façade facing east on Peachtree and the garden façade on the west; the latter elevation in form and detail is especially like the same aspect of Means's Shackelford house.

Means created his version of the Hunter Cooper house, using some of its salvaged parts; he saved a portion of Reid's great Michaelangelo-like columned frontispiece and reused it for the Shackelford entrance porch. The Hunter Cooper house had stood on the part of Peachtree in the vicinity of 25th and 26th streets, which was becoming commercial after having

Opposite: Entrance elevation and motor court. Above: Garden elevation.

been residential since the turn of the century. Reid's firm, Hentz, Reid & Adler, had designed the Peachtree (Brookwood) train station and six notable houses there, in an area once considered the most beautiful stretch of residential Peachtree. All of the houses are now gone. Means also used parts of another Brookwood house, the J. Carroll Payne of 1922, torn down in 1959, for another of his house projects. (See Dender house, page 50.)

As always with Means's domestic compositions, this is not a copy of another house, but an emulation of its aesthetic. Means's design is early-twentieth-century American neoclassical revival, Georgia school, the school's protégé, Jimmy Means, having become a master.

In addition to the Cooper house, Means also recalled in the Shackelford pedimented entrance façade Reid's limestone-clad Case house of 1919–21 on Habersham Road in Atlanta's Peachtree Heights Park. Homage to Neel Reid, too, are the first-floor French doors, one of Reid's favorite features.

This house that Means built for the Shackelfords captures the eclectic charm of the sophisticated domestic architecture that Reid and his colleagues brought to Atlanta early in the last century. "He Made Atlanta Beautiful" is the way an *Atlanta Journal* article about Neel Reid put it on March 1, 1963, when the Shackelford house was being designed. The article pictured the Hunter Cooper house with this caption, "Reid Creation at 1798 Peachtree Road will soon be demolished." That 1963 article said of Reid, "He never built a house without planning its garden." For the Shackelford house Means nearly duplicated Reid's Hunter Cooper garden façade, with the same projecting wings forming a rear terrace and using French doors around the first floor; thus he interrelated the house with the grounds, embowering it within a natural garden of trees. Means was called Neel Reid's hands; with this house he carried that tradition forward, literally, in his own practice, by this tribute to his old mentor.

Dr. and Mrs. Hutson Carspecken acquired the property in 1989 and commissioned Norman Askins to build a new pool house–office structure and a west addition with a master bedroom suite and garages on the lower level. Both the Carspeckens and their architect continued to respect and polish Means's homage to Reid, only adding to the special place this house holds among Means's works.

Shackelford-Carspecken House.
Opposite: Stair hall. Above: Library. Left: Living room.

BALLARD HOUSE

Means client: Mr. and Mrs. McCary Ballard.
Place: Atlanta. Completion Date: May 1965.
Style: Mid-eighteenth-century French pavilion.
Contractor/builder: Wesley Moran.
Millwork: Jim Girdler, W. P. Stephens Co., Marietta.
The Houses of James Means, *pp. 82–83.*

Means's fourth French house since 1956 is on the same quiet Atlanta street as the Marcus Cook house, completed in 1958. Comparing the two Buckhead houses reveals how James Means's genius for eclecticism itself, and in particular French neoclassical domestic architecture, allowed him a versatility and originality within the framework of the pavilion mode of Louis XV. This style was known for its intimate scale and emphasis on a comfortable but elegant domesticity. The pavilion was a domestic retreat from palace court life and, as such, was one of the sources of present-day suburban residential design.

The Ballard house is said to be inspired by a stylish pavilion, which was designed by the court architect Ange-Jacque Gabriel (1698–1782) and located in the village of Versailles, away from the palace. It was an example of the *noble simplicité* of mid-eighteenth-century French neoclassicism, as was Means's design for the McCary Ballards. Gabriel's genius was conservative, solid, unostentatious, refined, tasteful, much like that of James Means.

Gabriel's intimate domestic architecture, his world-famous pavilions, include the royal, incomparably elegant and refined Petit Trianon (1760s). Gabriel assimilated the lessons learned from the past. On principle, he emulated the beautiful time-tested precedents of classic architecture, much as did James Means.

Pavilion-sized neoclassical houses

had lower and simpler roofs than their predecessors, were more horizontal with less emphasis on the orders, curved elements, and carved ornamentation; basic geometry and pleasing proportions were more important than lavishness and "ritz." Pavilions were smaller-scale versions of the Italian villa, set in a garden landscape.

In 1962, as James Means was designing this and other French houses, an important book was published about this sort of domestic architecture, *Les Pavillons, "French Pavilions of the Eighteenth Century."* The text was by Cyril Connolly and the photographs by Jerome Zerbe. A photograph of one of the estate buildings at Gabriel's Pavilion du Butard, one of his first, is quite

Opposite: Entrance elevation. Below: Entrance (West) elevation drawing. Above: Living room.

Ballard House. Entrance/stair hall.

similar in scale and details to the garden façade of the Ballard house, especially the slate-covered mansard roof, eave-line dormers, and vine-covered trellis.

The Ballard entrance façade is more formal than the garden elevation, as it should be. Noble simplicity is expressed in the long, low, horizontal pediment and the symmetrical logic of the balanced pattern of windows, dormers, and central shuttered doorway. Here in Atlanta's Buckhead Means has embodied French neoclassicism at its reserved, refined, and well-proportioned best. It is set within the privacy and intimacy of a cobblestoned courtyard, behind a low wall in the front and a walled garden in the rear. There French doors, which are both windows and doors, bring the outdoors inside and punctuate the grey stucco with a sense of lightness, of light and nature embraced.

The Houses of James Means reported in 1979 that the Ballards' favorite room was the library "with its butternut (blond walnut) paneling." They considered that the outstanding interior feature was "the beautifully patterned wrought iron staircase" in the entrance stair hall just as one enters from the motor forecourt.

BALLARD HOUSE. Top: Library. Above: Rear (garden) exterior.

BARRETT-KUHLKE HOUSE

Means client: Mr. and Mrs. H. Gould Barrett.
Place: Augusta, Georgia. Completion Date: 1964.
Current Owner: Mr. and Mrs. F. Hamilton Kuhlke.
Style: Louisiana vernacular neoclassical.
Contractor/builder: J. C. Stockton & Son.
Millwork: Augusta Lumber Company.
Interim Owners: Mr. and Mrs. C. Dexter Jordan, Jr.
The Houses of James Means, *pp. 56–57.*

Below: Entrance elevation. Bottom: Entrance details.
Opposite: Entrance hall.

Founded in 1739, Augusta, the second-oldest city in Georgia (after Savannah) has many historic houses, especially from the nineteenth-century classical culture of white columns and fanlights. On a corner lot on a well-traveled street in the suburban Summerville area of Augusta stands a James Means house that he did for one of the Barretts, a notable Augusta clan. When their Means house was completed in 1964, it may have outdone all of this eighteenth-century city's fine old houses. Almost forty years later, it still endures as one of the most beautiful and distinctive ever built in this conservative town on the Savannah River (the hometown of the prestigious Augusta

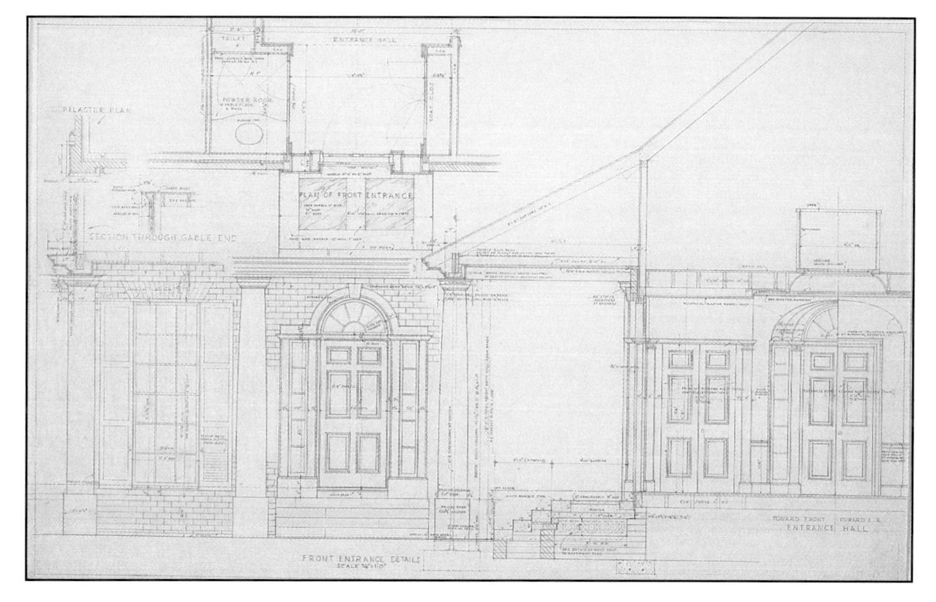

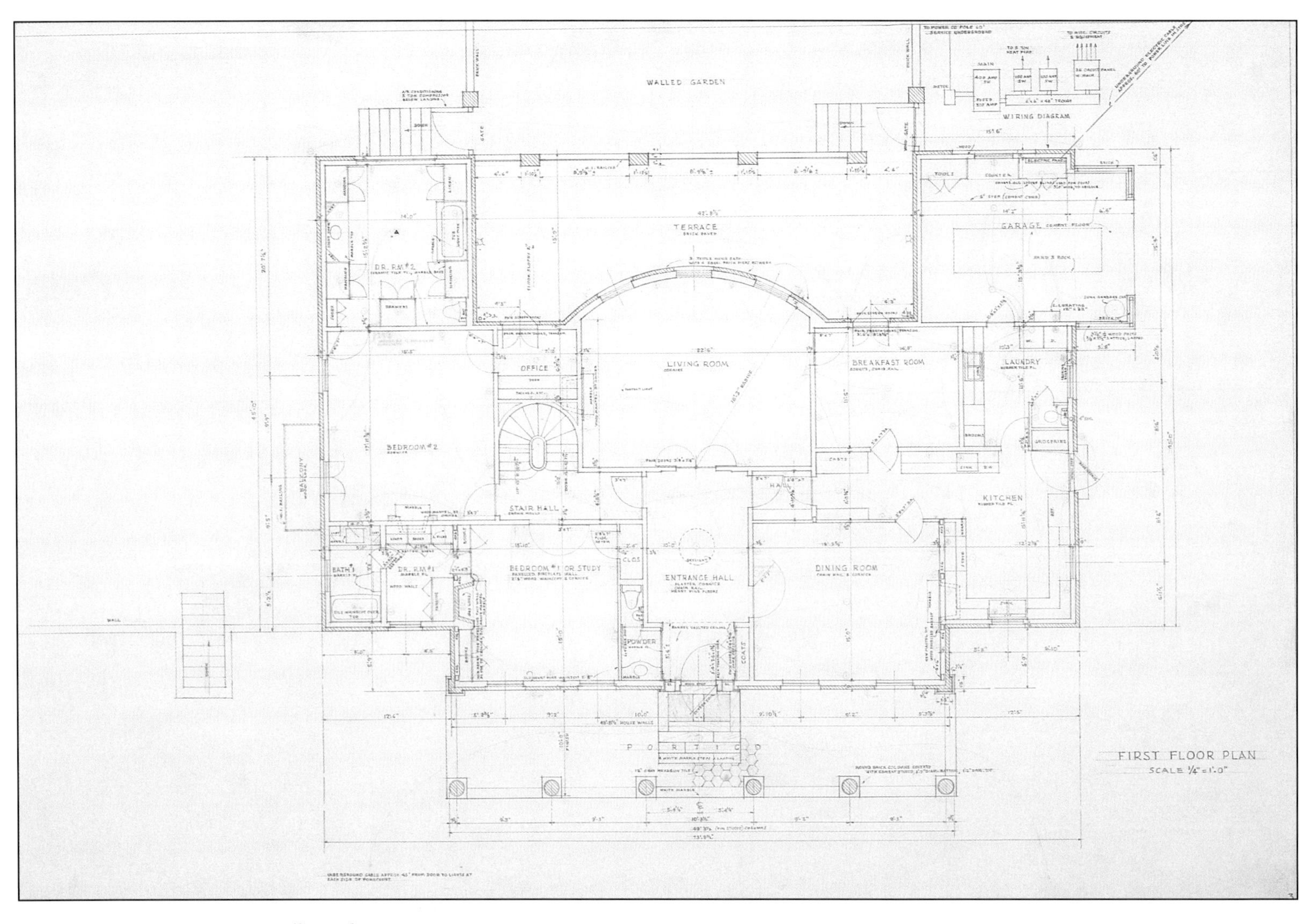

BARRETT-KUHLKE HOUSE. First floor plan.

National Golf Club and of its world-renowned Master's Tournament).

The precedent for the street elevation of this seemingly unique James Means house is an actual antebellum house that architect Edward Vason Jones photographed somewhere in Louisiana in the 1930s. Many copies of this photograph exist in the Edward Jones private archive in the Jones home in Albany, Georgia. Means evidently acquired a copy when he and Jones were partners in the early 1950s or when they were associated earlier on the staff of Hentz, Adler & Shutze. No exact data about the house, other than the haunting image itself, has been located. Means almost duplicated that piazza of six Tuscan columns resting on pedestals, which shelters a paved floor. Means's entrance façade design is intended as an identical twin of that one; the color of the stucco-over-brick columns, the Savannah grey bricks, and the buff-colored mortar joints seem to be Means's homage in spirit and tone to the house in the photograph.

For many years before their house was started, Mr. and Mrs. H. Gould Barrett collected architectural details, such as mantels, and other building materials, all of it from Georgia sites. Old Georgia heart pine, for example, was fashioned into a paneled den that was a favorite room of the Barretts and of their architect. One can see why. There are six old plantation mantelpieces throughout the house. In the dining room the Zuber handblocked wallpaper from France is still in place today.

Perhaps the most surprising architectural feature that we find behind this serene piazza with its simple fanlight is a spacious entrance rotunda and skylight oculus reminiscent of the work of the English neoclassicist Sir John Soane. Means has found just the right note of private glamour behind this quiet Southern vernacular portico.

The current owners, Mr. and Mrs. F. Hamilton Kuhlke, made it their own "historic" home in 1997; in their careful restoration they used some of the subcontractors from the original construction. Their intention has been to refurbish what Means and the Barretts originally achieved. Using the earth tones of the dining-room wallpaper as their palette, they have painted and furnished the interiors to complement the extraordinary style of the Means exterior and interior architecture. The result is now a landmark for our own day, to rival any important antique house in this old city (once called Fort Augusta) which sits astride the fall line, as the Savannah River slowly makes its way to the port city of Savannah and to the Atlantic Ocean beyond.

BARRETT-KUHLKE HOUSE. *Above: Study. Below: Exterior of living room bow window. Below right: Master bath.*

BARRETT-KUHLKE HOUSE: *Above: Living room. Right: Dining room.*

BRYANT-BRYANT HOUSE

Means client: Dr. and Mrs. Milton Bryant.
Place: Atlanta. Completion Date: July 1964.
Current Owner: Mr. and Mrs. Douglas W. Bryant (son and wife).
Style: Early American neoclassical vernaculars: Southern and Northern.
Contractor/builder: T. Thompson Construction Co.
Millwork: Jim Girdler, W. P. Stephens Co.
Later architect: Norman Davenport Askins.
The Houses of James Means, *pp. 52–53.*

Homeplace is not in a standard dictionary. Homestead is, and dates back to before the twelfth century. In Louisiana there is a house called Homeplace, the Pierre Gaillard house in St. Charles Parish, which dates from about 1800. The rear elevation of the Bryant house is quite like Homeplace, the traditional hip-roofed Louisiana plantation galleried form, with stout columns on pedestals on the first floor and slender columnettes on the second.

Southerners know and use the term homeplace, even if it isn't in the dictionary. We know a homeplace, the seat of a family, when we visit one. For the Bryants, their James Means house has become the home of a second generation. Jimmy Means designed such houses; people do not like to let them go. It is now the Bryant homeplace.

The current owner of the house, Douglas W. Bryant, turned four years old when his parents, Dr. and Mrs. Milton Bryant, moved in. He grew up here, and he and his wife, Nancy, became official keepers of the place in late 1997. Doug Bryant's mother says that her late husband, Dr. Bryant, loved their home. She says they started the process of building it in 1963. They met James Means through Dr. John Ellis, whose project had begun before theirs; the Ellises finished in March 1964, and the Bryants finished that July.

The front elevation owes an important architectural element to Mrs. Milton Bryant. She wanted a small classical porch; the first set of drawings had no porch. She found a photograph of just such a porch on an old house in New England, and she convinced Means to adapt it for her place. When asked what style their house was, she says, "Jimmy Means would tell people it was Yankee in the front and Southern in the garden."

The living room mantel that Means found for the Bryants in pieces at Charleston, South Carolina, was made in New England of Northern white pine, Means said, and he thought that combination was especially appropriate for their house.

Opposite: Entrance elevation.
Above: Front entrance details.
Right: Rear elevation and swimming pool.

Means did much of the restoration work on their antique neoclassical mantelpiece himself, with the help of a painter called Pop, who took off about fourteen layers of old paint.

The Bryants' favorite architectural feature of their homeplace is the spiral staircase in the spacious entrance hall. Its elegant geometrical simplicity epitomizes the taste of their architect, and one of its subtle details points to his understated, down-to-earth approach. The dentil molding ornamenting the end of each tread is left over from the living-room cornice. That use appealed to the elder Mrs. Bryant who had, she says, "a Scottish grandmother."

The younger generation Bryants

Bryant-Bryant House.
Above: Den. Left: Living room.
Opposite: Stair hall.

retained Atlanta architect Norman Askins, who has worked on numerous Means houses, to help them renovate the place for their tenure. That work was completed in 1999. Among the renovations were a new kitchen and butler's pantry, a new master bath and closets, one new child's bathroom, and a reworking of the attic.

The Bryant homeplace is the third Means house on the same street in Kingswood, a Buckhead neighborhood; the other two are French. Although the French do not have an exact word for homeplace, the other two houses have the potential for that comfortable Southern vernacular designation.

ELLIS HOUSE

Means client: Dr. John Oliver Ellis (1917–2000) and Gene Palfrey Ellis.
Place: Atlanta. Completion Date: March 1964.
Current Owner: Mrs. John Oliver (Gene Palfrey) Ellis.
Style: Southern vernacular neoclassical.
Contractor/builder: T. Thompson Construction Co.
Millwork: Jim Girdler, W. P. Stephens Co.
The Houses of James Means *pp. 50–51.*

Before the Ellises became clients of James Means, they had definite ideas about the style of house they wanted. They compiled a notebook of ideas. Their house would reflect their own family background, hers in Louisiana and his in South Carolina and Atlanta. Perhaps Atlanta won out because this is a Means Atlanta house, a merging of both their regional cultural traditions into a new design for an Atlanta neighborhood just off of West Paces Ferry Road in suburban Buckhead, where some of Atlanta's best domestic architecture has long been located.

A style term must be coined for their house; let us call it Southern vernacular neoclassical. The front elevation reflects both American and French Louisiana; note the pitch of the hipped roof, with a bit of Charleston federal in the fanlighted doorway, or perhaps such early American–era neoclassical houses in New Orleans as the Hermann-Grima house of the 1830s. The rear, or garden, elevation falls more purely into the tradition of the Louisiana plantation style down to the placement of the gallery staircase. (Think of famous galleried Louisiana houses such as Parlange and Homeplace.) Like the Ellises themselves, their Means house represents a happy marriage.

Opposite: Entrance elevation. Above: Rear elevation.

One important influence on the design was the great Louisiana house at New Iberia, the Shadows-on-the-Teche, now a house museum. The Shadows was in Gene Ellis's family; the last private resident of the Shadows was Weeks Hall, a cousin of hers and a great grandson of David Weeks, who built it about 1833. The Shadows, like the Means house of the Ellises, is also two-story brick, which synthesized both American and French Louisiana vernacular building ideas.

The Ellises owned the lot for a number of years before they decided on an architect. They had talked to architect Thomas G. Little before he died in a plane crash in 1962. Little was another very talented Georgian who did some wonderful Southern vernacular houses and several restorations after he had spent a long period on the staff of Colonial Williamsburg. The Ellises' thinking tended from the outset in the direction of an early Southern American house, which is why they chose James Means.

Mrs. Ellis recalled precisely that their house was begun on June 28, 1963, and that they moved in on March 11, 1964. She said, "I'd always loved pretty houses, and my father loved old houses." By working with Means they satisfied both aspects to achieve a pretty new house that seemed old, in the best possible sense, of classic.

Dr. Ellis, who died in January 2000, wrote for *The Houses of James Means* in 1979, "We think Mr. Means was not only an architect but an artist. His concept of design and proportion was exceptional." Among the old building materials that Means helped the Ellises accumulate was roof slate from an old college building in Macon, Georgia. Dr. Ellis already had on hand a batch of fireplace tiles they used from his mother's house that had stood at Peachtree Street and Ponce de Leon Avenue in Atlanta. Perhaps these materials are another reason why this is an Atlanta Southern house, as well as bayou Louisiana and "low-country," as they say in Charleston, South Carolina.

Ellis House.
Left: Entrance/stair hall.
Above: Library with view to stair hall.

FELKER-FELKER HOUSE

Means client: Mr. and Mrs. George W. Felker III.
Place: Monroe, Walton County, Georgia.
Completion Date: October 1964.
Current Owner: Mr. and Mrs. G. Stephen Felker (son and wife).
Style: Eighteenth-century Virginia Georgian.
Contractor/builder: Gabe B. Jarrard, Gainesville, Georgia.
The Houses of James Means, *pp. 32–33.*

Monroe, Georgia, the county seat of Walton County, is due east of Atlanta. The university town of Athens is just northeast in adjacent Clarke County. The Alcovy River flows through Walton County just west of Monroe, which is a textile town; among the busy mills is Avondale, with which the name Felker has long been synonymous.

James Means's Monroe clients, Mr. and Mrs. George W. (Lella) Felker III, moved into their home in the fall of 1964. The Felkers, originally Virginians, wanted a house reminiscent of the Old Dominion; they and their architect brought a beautiful and convincing bit of James River to the Alcovy. A new "home sweet home" was seldom sweeter.

The Felkers' Westerly stands at the very end of a picturesque street of handsome twentieth-century houses of quality and traditional design, set far back from the street on

Opposite top: Entrance elevation.
Opposite bottom: Living room from hall.
Right: Entrance/stair hall.
Below: Entrance/stair hall elevations.

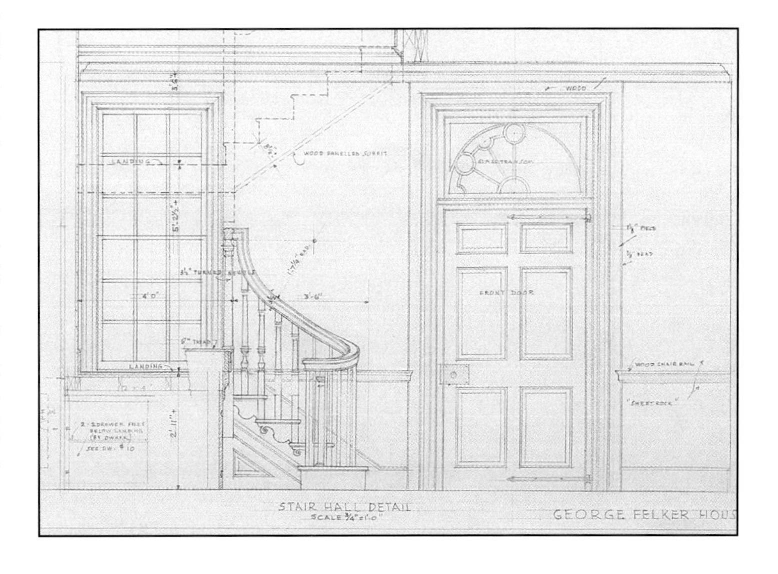

large lots. More secluded than the others, Westerly is atop a hill within numerous wooded acres; among its parklike features is a small lake, one of four with the magical Sanskrit names of childhood memory, "eney, meny, miny, moe."

Taking just over a year to build, Westerly seems to have been there for at least 200; James Means carefully designed and crafted it to that end. He was assisted by a Gainesville, Georgia, builder, Gabe Jarrard, who found old-fashioned workmen; five carpenters were particularly skilled. As always Means was the final arbiter. "Jimmy wouldn't like it" became the project byword and still remains a family standard among the older generation.

Mrs. George W. (Lella) Felker turned her Means house over to her son, Stephen Felker, and his wife, Christine, after the death of the patriarch Felker. Lella Felker, however, remained in residence in the neighborhood along the street leading to her old home. It is hard to leave a Jimmy Means house far behind.

With the passing years, the illusion that Westerly is a part of eighteenth-century Virginia becomes even more believable. Georgia classicist James Means always sought to fashion beauty that ages into its setting, as though always at home there. How appropriate, then, that a second generation of Felkers should enjoy passing through this timelessly beautiful neoclassical entrance porch, into a perfect, fanlighted stair hall with a gracious stairway, all of which together evoke the colonial Georgian period of old Virginia almost as well as the originals along the James.

That Monroe, Georgia, is named for Virginian James Monroe should not escape those of us who have been fortunate enough to pass over this threshold that James Means fashioned for transplanted Virginians in Walton County, Georgia, almost forty years ago.

PARKER HOUSE

Means client: Mr. and Mrs. William A. Parker, Jr.
Place: Atlanta. Completion Date: 1965; fire, 1974, major rebuilding as originally designed.
Style: Maryland Georgian colonial.
Contractor/builder: Joseph Walker, original builder, J. Ottwell Kelly, foreman, also for 1974 rebuilding, Cecil Malone Company.
Millwork: Jim Girdler, W. P. Stephens Co.
The Houses of James Means, *pp. 20–21; title page, Parker entrance doorway detail.*

Above: Entrance elevation.
Opposite top: Section interior details.
Opposite bottom: Rear elevation and swimming pool.

Nancy and Bill Parker completed their James Means house in 1965 after spending three years building it. Then in 1974 they practically had to start all over after a fire in part of the house required a major rebuilding. The original foreman, J. Ottwell Kelly, came back to oversee the reconstruction of the Means design as the architect had originally conceived it for the Parkers.

Said to be based on a hunting lodge from colonial Maryland, it is surrounded by acres of northwest Atlanta woods, which are, in fact, within the city limits. Another of Means's T-shaped plans, the Parkers' large, gambrel-roofed, antique salmon-pink brick colonial re-creation was a livable home for the Parkers' family of three children (now adult). The grounds with formal forecourt and boxwood gardens were also Means's design, but there is a swimming pool in the rear for informal family entertaining.

Much of the original interior decoration is still just as it was when the late classicist David Richmond Byers III helped the Parkers compliment Means's architecture in the 1960s and 70s. Because the plan of the house is one room deep, and there are many windows embracing the outdoors, the interiors are light filled and cheerful, even with its patrician ambience.

William A. Parker, Jr., commented to the author in late 1998 as this new James Means book was underway, "Jimmy Means was a unique person with a huge talent, a true artist, with an unfailing sense of proportion." After many years of residency here, the Parkers are obviously still among James Means's greatest fans. Testimony is the major rebuilding ten years after its completion to restore the house exactly as

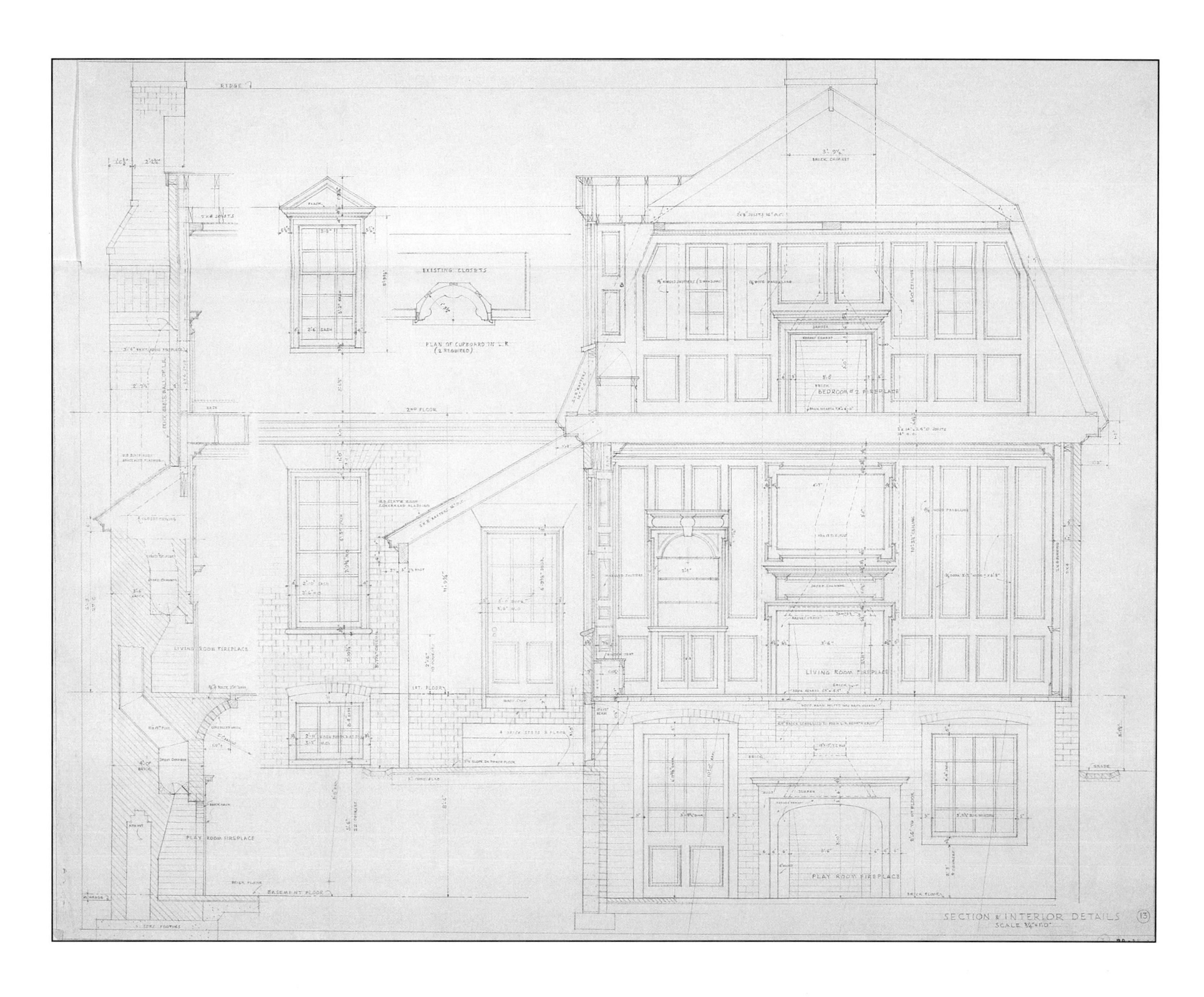

Means had designed it.

Bill Parker had come by his taste for classicism quite naturally. His father's Atlanta home, where he grew up, had been designed by another talented architect, Lewis Edmund Crook, Jr., a prominent member of Neel Reid's intimate circle in the Georgia school of classicists. Similarly Nancy Fraser Parker's love of the classic had been profoundly influenced by her own family's Neel Reid house, the Dorsey-Fraser house of 1924, at 2 Vernon Road in Atlanta's Peachtree Heights Park. Means was indeed fortunate to have had such knowledgeable and appreciative clients, who still reside in their Means house more than thirty-five years after they had it designed and built.

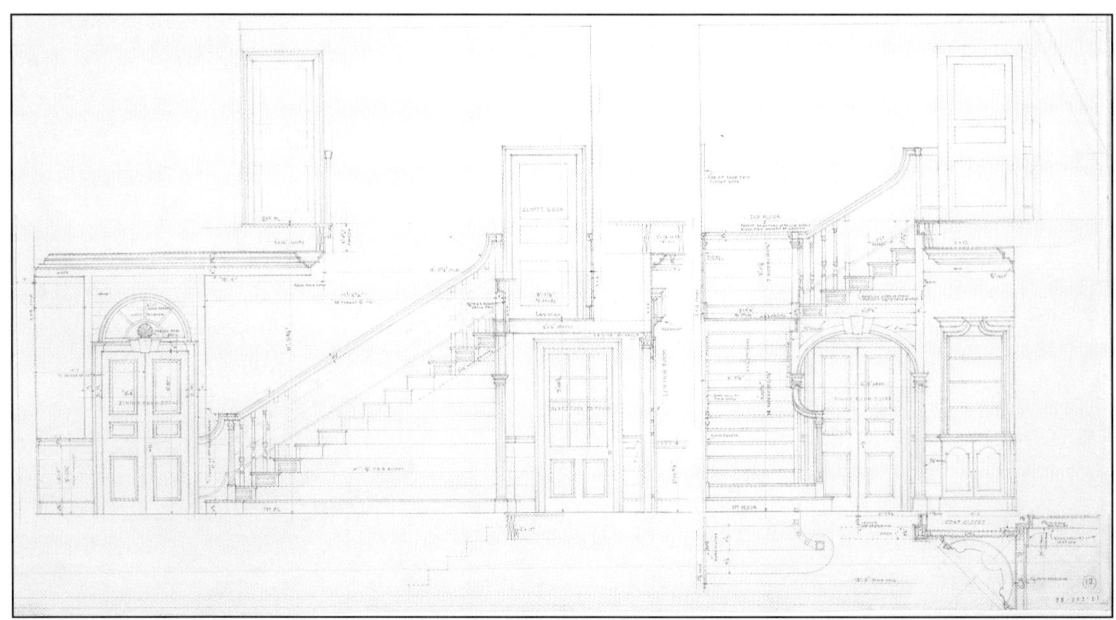

Parker House.
Above: Entrance/stair hall.
Right: Elevations of stair hall.

PARKER HOUSE.
Left: View from stair hall into study.
Below: First floor plan.

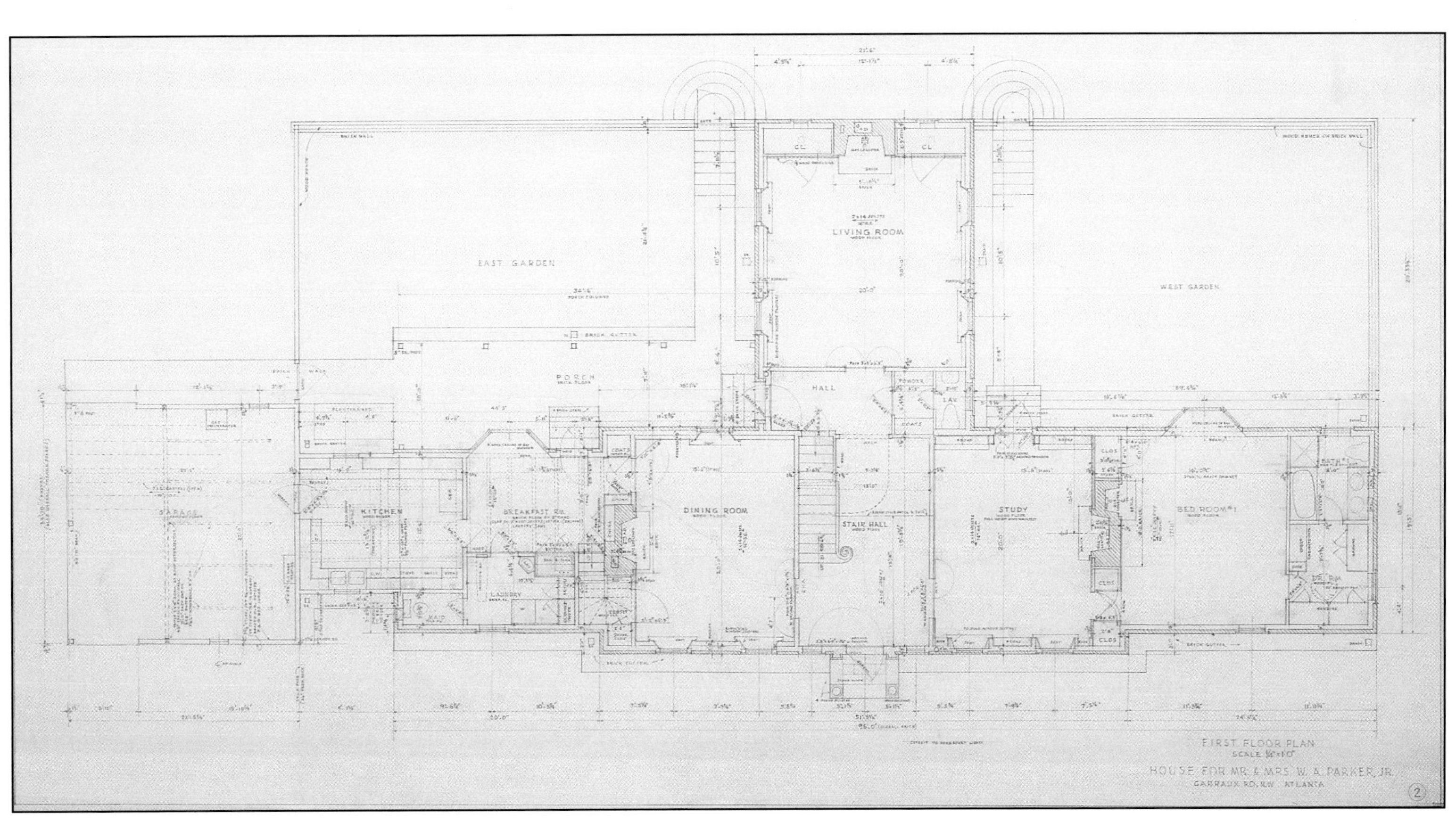

MARTIN HOUSE

Means client: Mr. and Mrs. Thomas E. Martin, Jr.
Place: Atlanta. Completion Date: 1966.
Style: Southern Georgian colonial.
Contractor/builder: Lewis Waldrop.
Millwork: Jim Girdler, W. P. Stephens Co.
The Houses of James Means, *pp. 36–37.*

Over a period of twenty years, this is the third time this author has written about Thomas E. and Peggy Sheffield Martin's James Means house in northwest Atlanta. First in 1981–82, for *Landmark Homes of Georgia*, and then in 1990–91 for *Classic Atlanta*, he placed their house in perspective among other significant examples of domestic architecture in Georgia and Atlanta. Ten years after the last account, the house is still the home of the Martin family, although Tom Martin died in the year 2000. This house is part of his legacy.

The first people with whom the author discussed this Means book were the Martins, in April 1998, at an Atlanta Botanical Garden event in the rose garden. Tom Martin beamed with pleasure and pride as he recalled his and Peggy's achievement in 1966 when they completed their home after almost two years of work. He remembered Jimmy Means's zeal in realizing a rare vision of Tidewater Virginia style they all wanted to achieve. Means was unwilling to cut corners, and the Martins found a way to satisfy his artistic standards. Many years later the wisdom of the collaboration with their demanding architect is apparent in the enduring beauty they created in the mid-1960s.

Means evoked for them the style of eighteenth-century James River plantations, which they both remembered from their days in Virginia colleges. The land on which Means sited the house, on axis with an oak tree that still stands at the rear elevation, was a rural-seeming place, two terraces above the south bank of Nancy Creek, exactly the sort of site that Means favored.

It is a country house in a suburban setting, reached by way of a gravel drive through meadowland that once was the scene of horseback forays by some neighbors who called their group the Saddle and Sirloin Riding Club. One of those neighbors sold the Martins the property that already had several old outbuildings, a bridge across the creek, and an old allée of oak trees. They added stables.

Means based the serpentine walled boxwood garden on Thomas Jefferson's

Opposite: Front entrance elevation.
Top: Rear entrance. Left: Dining room.

drawings for gardens at the University of Virginia. Souvenir bricks from Virginia plantation houses are inserted in the end wall of the south wing facing the garden. The main block of the house, with its balancing wings, is reminiscent of Carter's Grove and Westover. The arched doors and windows similar to those at Westover (c. 1734) are among the extra budgetary items on which Means insisted, as is the rubbed and gauged red brick for these arches. Such subtle touches work the architectural alchemy that transports one from Nancy Creek to the banks of the James.

Mrs. Martin and decorative arts specialist David Richmond Byers III collaborated in the original interior decoration to complement the Southern Georgian architectural style that Means rendered faithfully. Much of this interior decoration is still in place, for example, the chinoiserie wallpaper Mr. Byers had painted for the dining room.

Through uncurtained shuttered windows in the dining room one glimpses the unrivaled meadowland setting of one of James Means's largest private commissions. The late Thomas E. Martin, Jr., was quoted in *The Houses of James Means* as saying that the house was "a joy to research, design, and build." He had the added joy of living here for three-and-one-half decades.

MARTIN HOUSE.
Top: Stair hall. Above: Den. Opposite top: Living room. Opposite bottom: First floor plan.

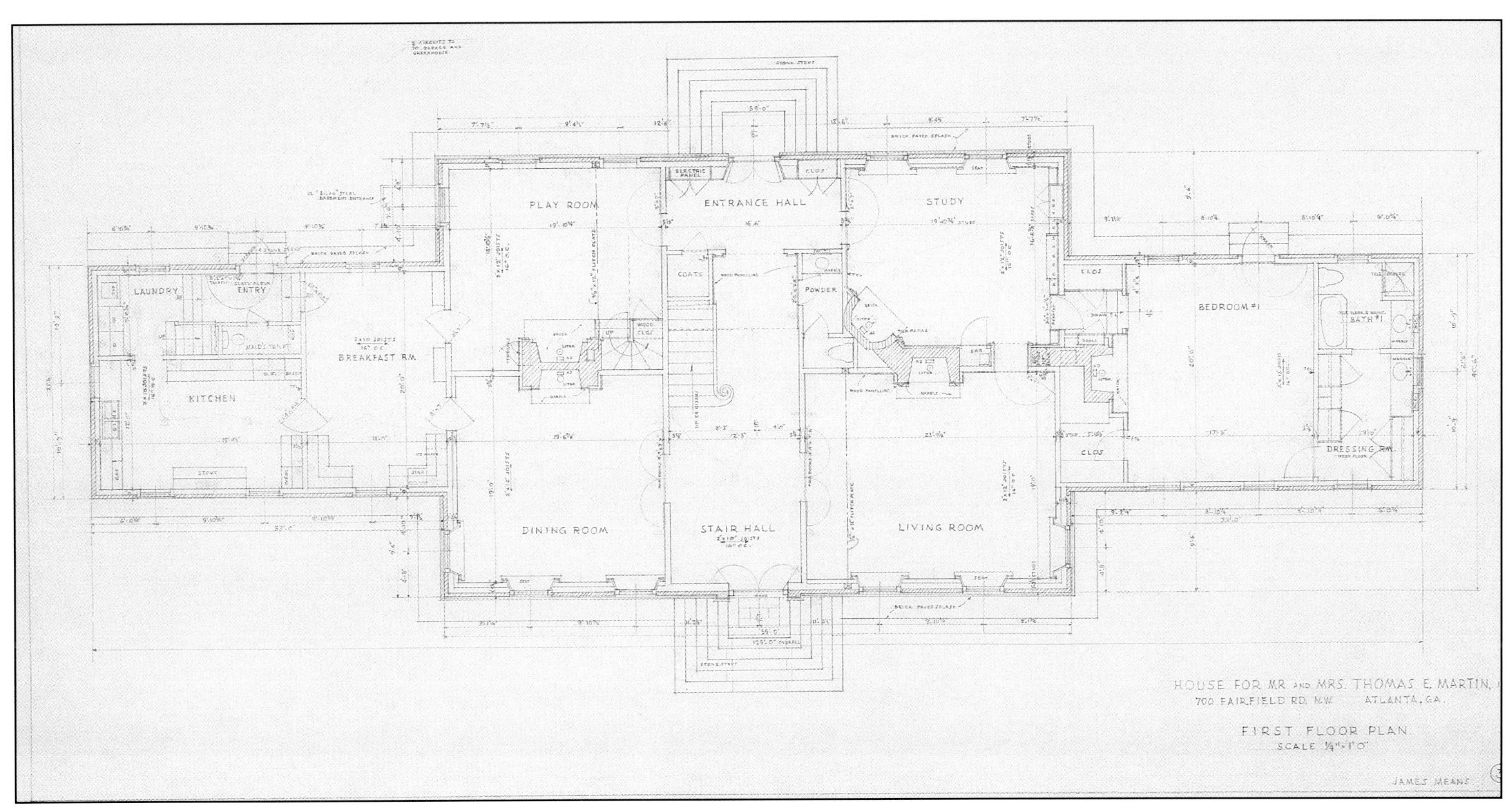
PLAY ROOM
ENTRANCE HALL
STUDY
LAUNDRY
ENTRY
BREAKFAST RM.
KITCHEN
COATS
POWDER
BEDROOM #1
BATH #1
CLOS
DRESSING RM.
DINING ROOM
STAIR HALL
LIVING ROOM
HOUSE FOR MR AND MRS. THOMAS E. MARTIN,
700 FAIRFIELD RD. N.W. ATLANTA, GA.
FIRST FLOOR PLAN
SCALE ¼"=1'0"
JAMES MEANS

PIKE HOUSE

Means client: Dr. and Mrs. John Sanders Pike.
Place: Marietta, Georgia. Completion Date: December 1966.
Style: Plantation plain-style, federal period.
Contractor/builder: Dan Brothers.
House Mover: Joe Slay.
The Houses of James Means, *pp. 92–93.*

Above: Front exterior.
Opposite: Library mantel.

Southern Accents magazine in the winter of 1984 spread this James Means project before its readers as "A Loving Restoration, the Hill-Pike House in Cobb County, Georgia." The article told the story of a house moved from Washington- Wilkes, Georgia, and renovated as an Atlanta restaurant, which inspired Dr. J. Sanders (Sandy) Pike, a dentist, and his wife, Mary, to attempt a similar undertaking as a home for themselves.

They found that another house from Georgia's Washington needed saving. The John Hill house stood empty on the side of the courthouse square. It was a seven-room federal period, plantation-plain-style dwelling begun in 1788, enlarged in 1819 with a central hall, and enlarged again in 1835. The Pikes had it moved in two sections, the top floor and the bottom, 120 miles to the middle of a wooded nine-acre plot in Cobb County, with a Marietta, Georgia, mailing address. The Pikes say they "bought four more houses to do one," so as to have all the old parts they needed. One of the houses cost fifty dollars at the time; their red library came from that house.

James Means helped supervise the Hill house dismantling and the move, protecting the beaded weatherboards, the original heart-pine floors, old window glass, and the original 1788 staircase. The Pikes followed the truck at

OKLAHOMA
MISTLETOE

Pike House.
Above: Living room.
Left: Rear elevation and garden.

ten miles an hour. Hill house was in a natural state; it had never had electricity, plumbing, or central heat, all of which were added without harming its historic integrity. Not a single piece of new building material was used in the restoration, which included 31,000 pre–Civil War bricks.

A year of hard work was required for client and architect to shape the dream. It is like the Pikes' child; James Means was the godfather. One of his admonitions was "not to over-furnish it," to which the Pikes replied, "We can easily do that!" Mary Pike's expert needlework brightens the place and affirms what a personal and loving restoration the Hill-Pike house has been. The Pikes are an adventurous couple who tracked down, with Jimmy

Means, every old pine board, handmade brick, and nail to give their adopted child a better life 120 miles from where it was born in Washington-Wilkes, Georgia.

The author visited Hill-Pike house in 1971 with James Means, the proud godparent of this private restoration-renovation, which had followed his public Stone Mountain Plantation project of the early 1960s. (See pages 14 and 27). Our visit came when both of us were on the Tullie Smith House Committee for the restoration of an 1830s plantation-plain-style house that had been moved to the grounds of the Atlanta Historical Society. Some thirty years later the Hill-Pike house still shines, reflecting great credit on its adoptive parents.

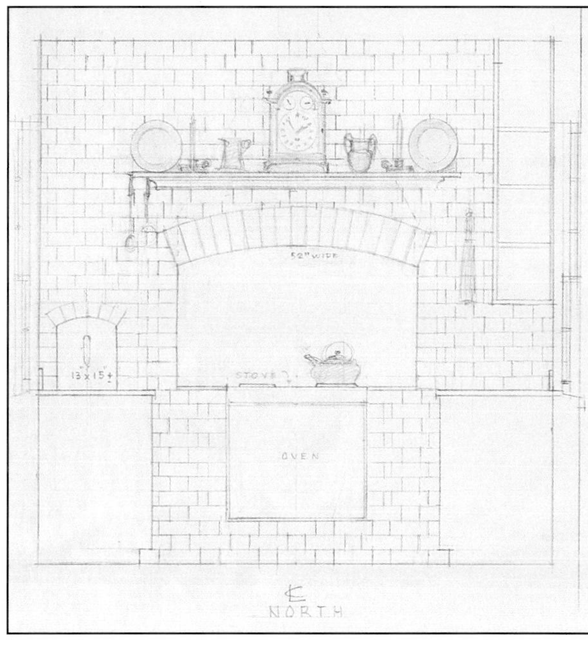

PIKE HOUSE. Above: Kitchen oven. Left: Elevation drawing of kitchen oven.

TORRENCE HOUSE

Means client: Mr. and Mrs. Samuel M. Torrence, Jr.
Place: Dothan, Alabama. Completion Date: July 1966; Askins addition, 1996.
Style: Southern vernacular.
Contractor/builder: Sam Torrence; carpenter foreman, Elton Monday.
Millwork: Perry Clark.
Later architect: Norman Davenport Askins.
The Houses of James Means, *pp. 54–55.*

Architects of the Georgia school of classicists sometimes placed formal entrance façades, for privacy and surprise, away from the street; a more informal, sometimes a garden, side becomes the first aspect seen as one approaches the house. For this hidden front, there is often a motor forecourt reached from an encircling drive. (Neel Reid's Dorsey-Fraser house, in Atlanta's Buckhead suburb, pictured on the cover of *Classic Atlanta,* is an example.)

James Means's Sam Torrence house in Dothan, Alabama, completed in the summer of 1966, is a contribution to that reverse arrangement: a frame Louisiana or low-country two-story gallery elevation toward the street and a formal, eighteenth-century red-brick Virginia Georgian–style main entry façade, with a handsome fanlighted frontispiece, secluded in the rear. Although Means's Ellis and Bryant houses are not built according to this reverse scheme, they are similar in character in that one side is brick and strictly symmetrical and the other is more casual, galleried, low country, Southern.

Floor-length windows and French doors open onto the wide galleried porch from the living, dining, and breakfast rooms. This plan is similar to the Louisiana Creole plan, where the galleries were like another room, an outside hall providing connections between rooms in a warm climate where shaded outdoor living has been typical, especially before the days of Sunbelt air-conditioning.

The *Houses of James Means* catalogued interesting sources for Torrence building materials: beams for the down-

Above: Entrance elevation.
Left: Family room.

stairs playroom came from an old piano store, c. 1880, in downtown Atlanta; bricks, from the 1859 courthouse at Cleburne County, Alabama; stair balusters, from the first Houston County, Alabama, courthouse; roof slate, from a building at the University of Georgia, Athens. Wide Florida cypress boards were used downstairs and upstairs, in porch floors, railings, steps, and interior shutters. The Torrence family's favorite room has been the library, with deep blue paneling and a corner fireplace with a Dutch tile surround, often a James Means feature.

Sam Torrence was his own contractor, and he and his family are still pleased with his and Jimmy Means's handiwork down in deep southwest Alabama at Dothan, about equidistant from the Georgia and Florida boundaries. The Torrence place seems right at home here but is no less outstanding in the neighborhood for its rare and distinctive architectural qualities. Atlanta architect Norman Askins respected these when in 1996 he added a new frame master bedroom/bathroom wing to the entrance side. It looks every bit at home here as did the Means original.

Torrence House. Opposite: Garden exterior.
Top: Rear elevation. Above right: Living room.

BOUNDS-BOUNDS HOUSE

Means client: Mr. and Mrs. Osborne Bounds, Jr.
Place: Washington, Wilkes County, Georgia. Completion Date: Fall 1968.
Current Owner: Mr. and Mrs. Lincoln H. (Cindy Russell) Bounds (son and wife).
Style: Federal period Plantation-plain (restoration).
Contractor/builder: Dan Brothers, Marietta, Georgia, and L.C. Holden, Atlanta.
The Houses of James Means, *pp. 94–95.*

Washington, Georgia, the county seat of Wilkes County, is known as Washington-Wilkes to distinguish it from the national capital. It was the first town in America chartered in the name of the general (and later founding father), January 23, 1780. It is difficult to write enough to describe the collected beauty of the neoclassical houses there. One reason Medora Field Perkerson called her popular book *White Columns in Georgia* (1952) is because of places like Washington in the piedmont of Georgia; Perkerson described it as "this charming antebellum town of white-columned houses."

Osborne Bounds Jr. was part and parcel of Washington-Wilkes; his family was among the largest landowners—he was deeply rooted here. He once told this author that he returned home because it was "the path of least resistance." His wife, Barbara, was a New Englander, which is not so far-fetched, because Washington-Wilkes could be a gracious Southern version of a picturesque and tidy Connecticut town.

During 1964–66, with copies of Frederick Nichols's *Early Architecture of Georgia* (1957) convenient, Osborne Bounds and some of his cousins and other antiquarian-minded folk, including this author, spent weekends rambling among the area's old houses, of which there were scores. This historic up-country region of Georgia was the earliest to be settled west of Augusta and the Savannah River before and during the American Revolution. On those rambles we first saw the two houses,

Right: Entrance elevation. Above: Front entrance porch details.

Bounds-Bounds House. Above: Living room. Opposite: Side and rear.

the Graves and the Wingfield, both c. 1800, from which the Bounds house was composed.

Attractive country, it was (and is) a far frontier of British America that had had to be defended to establish independence. The general's name became the name of the town because Washington-Wilkes became a stronghold of patriots building and defending their homes. That independent-minded tradition has held here in the vicinity of the Battle of Kettle Creek, a 1779 patriot victory over the Tories that caused the British to abandon Augusta and this part of the Georgia frontier. The Washington-Wilkes homes defended then have become its glory and, perhaps, its greatest heritage. Home tours are an honored part of community life.

Osborne Bounds Jr. decided to add a new home to the tradition, but one that would seem to have been there all along, literally, going back to the federal, pre–Greek revival culture of the early settlers from Virginia and the Carolinas and later the Revolutionary War soldiers who took up generous land bounties. The front portion of the house was originally the home of the Wingfields, who moved to Wilkes County in 1784, and is given a turn-of-the-century federal period date of c.1800. This Wingfield portion, which had become a barn but was intact, with its original faux graining and marbleizing, was moved to its current 200-acre site south of the town square in 1964; Osborne had it placed on a knoll above two creeks. The area was once called Mineral Springs. The back portion of the composition was moved in 1966 from the French Mills section of the county. It was originally the home of Col. John Graves, a Revolutionary War soldier, and of his son, Dr. John T. Graves.

Osborne Bounds, a knowledgeable, understated gentleman quite naturally chose James Means as the architect to help him. For *The Houses of James Means*, in which it was called, "A House in Northeast Georgia," Bounds wrote: "Mr. Means' skill and taste were responsible for the very few necessary changes. . . . (His) taste and understanding were of such help in seeing that the

right kind of work was done. Any other architect would have wanted changes that really would not have been improvements."

When the current owner, Lincoln Bounds, Bobbie and Osborne's son, was still a baby, this author spent a night in the house because he had to give a lecture to the local historical society. The feeling one had was that the Bounds house was a Japanese teahouse in which one padded reverently about, without shoes, to protect the sacred heart-pine floorboards. Actually, Osborne Bounds was charming in the way he loved the place that he and Means had fashioned from old houses and materials.

The perfectly scaled and proportioned, appropriately understated, vernacular federal entrance portico that Means designed, based on early county examples from the area, was seldom used; one usually entered from the side porch into a glazed sun porch next to one of the tall outside brick chimneys characteristic of the frame plantation-plain style houses of piedmont plateau Georgia. Both the Wingfield and Graves houses had most of the original British Carpenter-brand locks, augmented by others gathered from Wilkes and surrounding counties, including Oglethorpe and Lincoln.

It is said that Lincoln Bounds is named for that neighboring county and its Revolutionary War General Benjamin Lincoln, not for the Civil War president, Abraham. After all, this is a regional house, rooted in the land and culture surrounding it, also surrounded by vestiges of the father's native plant collection. Osborne Bounds, Jr., was a native son, and the local botany was one of his many interests; he knew Washington-Wilkes like the back of his hand. This house represented for him a "path of least resistance" back to his native soil. James Means understood and helped him achieve that honorable and deep-felt goal.

STEWART HOUSE

Means client: Mr. and Mrs. John G. Stewart.
Place: Gastonia, North Carolina. Completion Date: August 1968.
Style: American Georgian colonial revival.
Contractor/builder: Taylor Construction Company, Lenore, North Carolina.
The Houses of James Means, *pp. 40–41.*

Opposite: Front entrance.
Below: Entrance elevation and motor court.

James Means's genius for understated classic eclecticism is well demonstrated by the John G. Stewart house of 1968 in Gastonia, North Carolina. Means, with subtle creativity, harmonized numerous American Georgian– style elements from classic precedents into an original design, a new synthesis. *The Houses of James Means* said that it "epitomizes the beautiful qualities of James Means' work."

Mrs. Stewart's late father, who was a student of early American architecture and the building arts and found Mr. Means for the project, worked closer with Means than the Stewarts did themselves. Today, a bit more than thirty years later, the Stewarts feel privileged to continue to call this classic house their home.

Means laid down the gauntlet from the first element of the design that people encounter, the frontispiece entrance doorway, which is derived from that at the Wentworth-Gardner House in Portsmouth, New Hampshire. Typical of Jimmy Means, the Stewart front entrance is not an exact quotation from that famous precedent from coastal New England, a house that is said to represent the very peak of the colonial period in America. Its scrolled, or broken, pediment, featuring a symbolic pineapple (for hospitality) and supported by Corinthian pilasters, is part of a façade that has been under the protection of the Society for the Preservation of New England Antiquities since the 1930s.

Prosperous Portsmouth was known for the serene façades of its colonial houses that emphasized fine materials, superb carpentry, and fine detail. That description fits Means to the minute. Means had, in fact, stepped down the splendor of the Wentworth-Gardner doorway one notch by making his pilasters Ionic, instead of Corinthian.

Stewart House. Opposite: Stair hall. Above: Living room. Below: Stair hall detail.

One could never describe a Means house as ostentatious, nor the American Georgian houses of Portsmouth. The Stewarts' doorway frontispiece, with its carved mahogany pineapple, is about as rich as it gets, with Means or in Portsmouth.

But Means did not just adapt from New England for the Stewart house. He made quotations, at least in spirit, from Gadsby's Tavern in Alexandria, Virginia, for the living room mantel and chimney breast; from Claremont Manor in Surry County, Virginia, the dining room mantel; and from the Whitford house in New Bern, North Carolina, the chimney breast. From the John Stuart house in Charleston, South Carolina, came the downstairs over-door pediments. The wide stair hall, with its sweeping spiral, is divided by a screen of two fluted Doric columns reminiscent of the entrance hall of Clivedon in Philadelphia (1760s).

The Stewart house is a Means virtuoso performance of Georgian colonial style with modified citations of precedents from New England to the Carolinas. The entire property is surrounded by a handmade brick Jeffersonian serpentine wall. One enters the grounds between dignified brick piers with sculpted eagles setting the historical tone and enframing the elegant doorway ahead. Its carved pineapple seems to suggest that here is Southern hospitality of the old school we dream might still exist someplace as perfectly beautiful as the John Stewarts, Means house in Gastonia.

STEWART HOUSE.
Left: Dining room.
Above: Rear.

SHAPARD HOUSE

Means client: Mr. and Mrs. Robert P. Shapard III.
Place: Griffin, Spalding County, Georgia. Completion Date: 1969.
Style: Southern neoclassical.
Contractor/builder: Owners, with master carpenter Frank Gossett.
Millwork: Jesse Jones, Cornelia, Georgia.
The Houses of James Means, *pp. 46–47.*

Parallels between the Robert Shapards' ten-year architectural adventure in Griffin, Spalding County, Georgia, and the long-term building of Thomas Jefferson's Monticello near Charlottesville, Virginia, are not farfetched. They help tell a fascinating story unique among those of building the Means houses. The ten-year span for the Shapards' building project, 1959–69, although not quite as protracted as Jefferson's Monticello, is in the same realm of stages and persistence: Jefferson started Monticello in May 1768, in his twenty-fifth year, completing first one outbuilding, a one-room bachelor cottage, and fourteen years later completing the first phase. He then remodeled, enlarging and altering, for thirteen years. As Jefferson once wrote, "Architecture is my delight."

Virginia (Ginger) and Robert (Bobby) Shapard met James Means when they were twenty-three and twenty-eight, respectively, just as Jefferson had also been in his twenties when he began his Monticello adventures. The Shapards

Left: Approach to the entrance. Above: Entrance/stair hall.

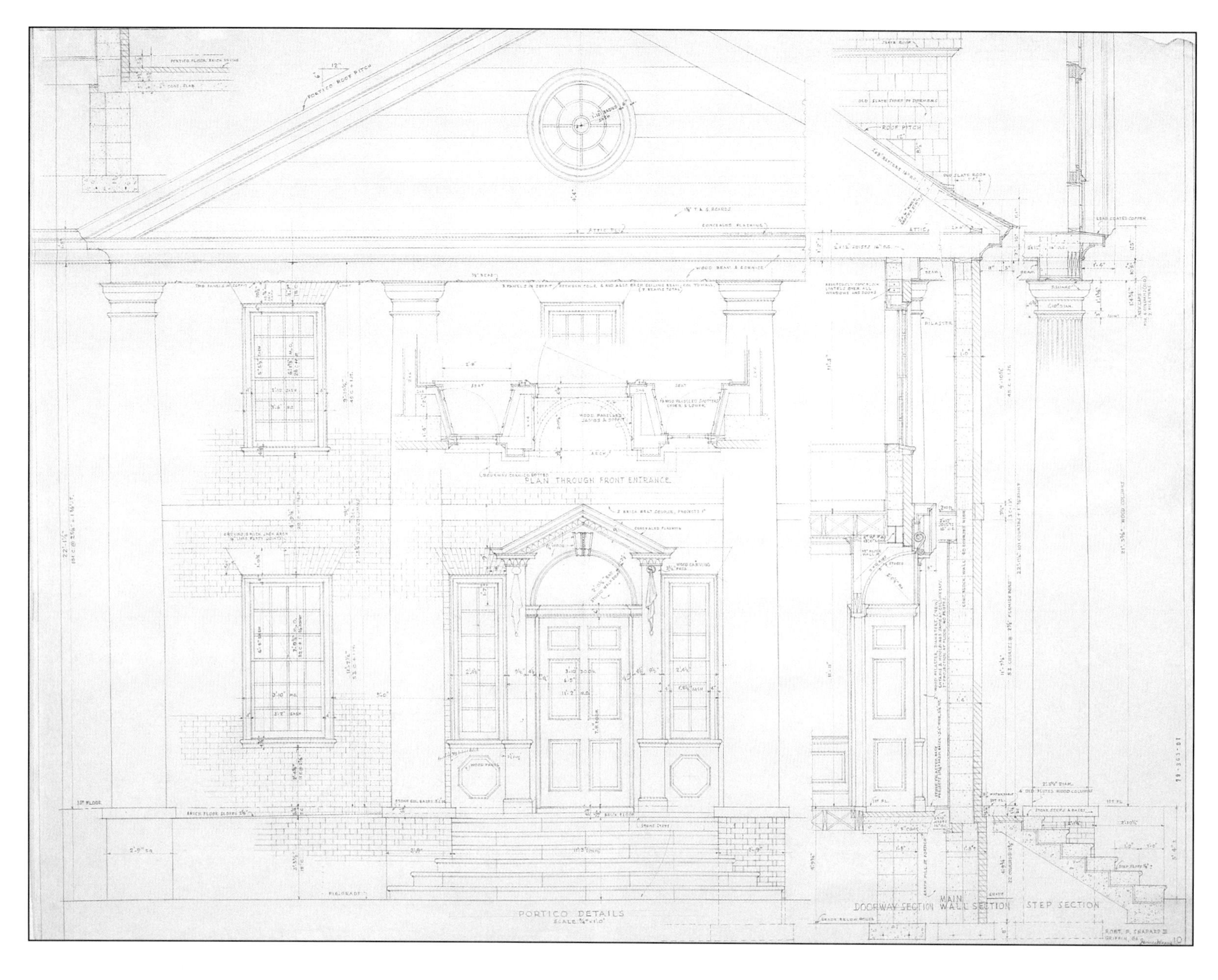

SHAPARD HOUSE. Above: Portico details. Below: Distant view of house and setting. Opposite: Entrance detail.

were next-door neighbors of the Will Plowdens in the College Street neighborhood of Griffin in the mid 1950s during the building of the Plowdens' Means house, which was completed in 1958. (See page 38.)

The Shapards started looking for property out from town in the country in 1959. After they had found their acreage (today a total of 204) Means came down to see the land and help select an exact building site on a hill with a sweeping view of distant hills and woods, sloping south-southwest toward a rural highway. To create a flat building area, later they would have to reconfigure the hill. This elevation would be the "mont" of their Monticello.

Shapard House. Living room.

After meeting Means the Shapards toured the state of Virginia with Thomas T. Waterman's *The Mansions of Virginia* (1952) as their guidebook. (Virginia Muller Shapard is a graduate of Randolph-Macon Woman's College in Lynchburg, Virginia, and her family was from the Norfolk area.) One of the places they visited was Mount Airy (the Tayloe house), which had also taken about ten years to complete, from 1748 to 1758. The overall layout of the north façade of that neo-Palladian plantation house provided for the Shapards and their architect the entrance façade scheme: a temple-fronted main block and flanking dependencies projecting forward, with a semicircular drive below and a low terrace with a forecourt raised above, reached by low steps that are flanked by carved urns on pedestals.

Mount Airy and other houses with the Palladian villa five-part plan became their model. The Shapards have never built, however, the planned hyphens or connecting passageways from the house to the flanking outbuildings, two of the parts of such a five-part layout.

The flanking dependencies, a garage and guest house, were the first parts constructed, along with the terrace with limestone urns and pedestals. The Shapards lived in this guest house for five years during construction of the first phases of the main house. This, too, parallels Jefferson's Monticello, where construction began with a brick dependency on the site, the honeymoon cottage, providing a place to live and important experience in the art of building. This certainly was the case with the Shapards, who were their own contractors. A master carpenter, Frank Gossett, assisted and supervised.

These dependencies set the style with hipped slate roof, windows with cherry-red jack arches (rubbed and gauged bricks), Flemish bond above the water table, and English bond below. All bricks came from the Locker Brick Company in Glascow, Virginia, which made the wood-molded bricks for Colonial Williamsburg, Inc.

Other Jeffersonian aspects are the neoclassicism of the main façade, similar to the white-columned, temple-like pavilions on the lawn at the University of Virginia, and the materials and coloring of red brick and white trim. This is the same red-and-white coloring of Monticello and of much else that Jeffer-

Shapard House. Dining room.

son designed and built, including Poplar Forest.

The Shapards' design is a quintessential Southern neoclassical house (with Georgian colonial overtones), but created in the last half of the twentieth century. Old materials were used almost exclusively, helping to give authenticity to the illusion that one is experiencing a house that has stood in place in Spalding County since long before the county was established in 1851.

The four fluted Greek-revival columns shining on their hill (above their twelve-acre lake just to the west side of the property) were originally from the Michael house in Athens, Georgia. Today, these have been replaced with redwood duplicates, because the old ones began to deteriorate. This weakening will not happen to the structure itself, for it is old heart pine, as are the flooring, exterior millwork, and unpainted portions of the interior millwork. The bold baroque stairway, inspired by those at houses in Virginia such as Carter's Grove, is also heart pine.

Designed to be appreciated as a work of architectural art from both far and near, it functions well visually from both perspectives. When one actually reaches the pediment portico, with its Georgian-style entrance frontispiece, one is greeted by Herbert J. Millard's handcarved drapery details on either side of the doorway. (Millard was one of the greatest artist-craftsmen in the Georgia school of classicists.) Straight ahead through the broad hallway is a garden or rear entrance with a fan-shaped transom, and above that a fine Palladian window lights the stair landing.

In *The Houses of James Means*, Virginia Shapard commented: "The scale, proportion, detail of design and millwork, grace and symmetry of our home is the product of the genius of James Means. He enjoyed watching the building grow over a protracted period of time and shared with us our joy, pride of work and participation in the project."

Thomas Jefferson's accomplishments at Monticello, his delight in architecture as a fine art, parallel the Shapards' experience in creating their own home near Griffin, where they still reside forty years after they first came to the site when they were young marrieds in their twenties. They say their children helped "antique" the place; now their grandchildren do.

MILNER-CANDLER HOUSE

Means client: Mr. and Mrs. Gene W. Milner.
Place: Atlanta. Completion Date: October 1970.
Current Owner: Mr. and Mrs. Walker T. Candler.
Style: Maryland Georgian revival.
Contractor/builder: Cecil Malone.
Millwork: Jim Girdler, W. P. Stephens Lumber Co.
Later architect: Norman Askins, 1987; Walker Candler.
The Houses of James Means, *pp. 26–27.*

Below: Entrance elevation. Opposite: Living room.

The Buckhead section of suburban northwest Atlanta began to be developed just before and after World War I. It was an expansive acreage that soon began to be subdivided into large building plots. Two great country-house estates were built facing each other on West Paces Ferry Road. One of these was Arden, the James Dickey house, which is still a landmark presence, Mount Vernon–like, on the south side of West Paces Ferry across from the present Georgia Governors Mansion. Arden was being designed and built by Hentz, Reid & Adler when James Means went to work for the firm in 1917.

The Gene W. Milner house stands on a hill on Arden Road where the stable had been for the original Dickey-Arden estate. Means designed a Southern, Georgian-style gambrel-roofed house similar to the sort that would have stood in mid-eighteenth-century rural Chesapeake Bay Maryland. The orange-red handmade Virginia brick, laid up with mortar colored with red Georgia clay, seems to tie it to the soil of its Atlanta location.

This Buckhead mansion is deceptively large and spacious, though modest in scale and aspect when viewed from Arden Road. A surprise comes upon entering the generous entrance hall with a stairway in an L shape to the rear. It is Tidewater in spaciousness and detail, imaginatively removing the

host and his guests into a pre-twentieth-century world of quiet elegance, only a few miles from the bustling shopping malls along Atlanta's Peachtree Road corridor.

The present owners of the Means Milner house of 1970, Mr. and Mrs. Walker (Mary Jane) Candler, have made it their own with some handsomely unobtrusive improvements that Walker Candler, a residential designer, found necessary because of changing times and his growing family's needs. Remodeling the kitchen and creating a family room from a rather plain playroom was a priority.

The Milners had added a swimming pool and neoclassical cabana as Buckhead lifestyles evolved. Norman Askins designed the cabana as the Milners requested, to relate less to Means's original exterior than to the open spaciousness of the interior; the casual openness of the columned loggia accomplished the goal of shelter by the side of the swimming pool, with neoclassical style (not unlike that of the nearby Dickey house) when viewed from the glazed rear porch. Candler enlarged the master bedroom suite, extending a wing on the north side of the rear that balances that toward the south.

Because James Means had worked for Neel Reid when that firm did the Dickey house he came home to the Arden property when he built the Milner house at the beginning of the 1970 decade. The Walker Candlers are at home here to stay and raise their family. Both the Candlers are that rare Buckhead Atlanta breed, natives with long community roots. They appreciate the tradition that Means's architecture has represented locally, with the changing generations and the tradition in Southern architectural style that Means's designs represented even when they were brand-new additions to the best domestic architecture of suburban Buckhead. The city's finest examples of the builder's art, James Dickey's neighboring Neel Reid–designed Arden among them, have long been concentrated in the northern suburbs.

Walker Candler was a founding director of Southern Architecture Foundation, Inc., publisher of this book.

MILNER-CANDLER HOUSE.
Left: Stair hall. Above: Dining room. Below: Rear exterior with swimming pool.

MOORE-CLARK HOUSE

Means client: Dr. and Mrs. B. Waldo Moore.
Place: Atlanta. Completion Date: November 1971.
Current Owner: Dr. and Mrs. Michael Clark.
Style: Charleston Georgian.
Contractor/builder: W. Byron Parker.
Millwork: Jim Girdler, W. P. Stephens Lumber Co.
Later architect: Keith Summerour, kitchen remodeling and new garage for the Clarks.
The Houses of James Means, *pp. 58–59.*

Dr. Waldo Moore and James Means were friends with mutual antiquarian interests, especially in collecting antiques and decorative arts. Moore also was one of Means's physicians. Fortunately, some of Means's comments about the Moore house were recorded when *The Houses of James Means* was produced in 1979. Means described the house he designed for Dr. Moore as "a type of Charleston, Georgian, eighteenth-century [house] with the main floor above a full basement and a double flight of stone steps up to a landing at the front door." Means was describing an urban townhouse form such as the William Gibbes house, built in Charleston about 1780, a sophisticated clapboard dwelling built, like the Moore house, on a high basement with twin flights of steps, handsome iron railings, and an imposing entrance frontispiece.

Located on a cul-de-sac of houses on lots subdivided from the large property at the rear of the James Dickey house, Arden, the Neel Reid–designed "Atlanta Mount Vernon" on West Paces Ferry Road, this brick manor house is a simple two-story block on a slight elevation facing south. The pattern of sash windows with jack arches and rubbed and gauged red brick is identical front and back, even down to the side windows at the front entrance and rear Palladian window. The orange-red brick color is quite similar to that on the nearby Milner-Candler house, also built on part of the old Dickey-Arden property.

Means harmonized outside and inside architecture with a repeated theme of broken pediments over mantelpieces and doors. On the rear façade he played on the geometry of arches, a satisfyingly symmetrical little neo-Palladian sonata.

Means wrote about the plan in 1979, "A generous stairway with a broad landing is lighted by a Palladian window." This large, arched window is seen on the rear elevation as a part of the play of arches. Brightly lit by many windows, the spacious stair hall at the center of the plan, with two large rooms on each side, becomes an additional living room, which is the way such spaces were used by eighteenth-century Southern families, as a sort of interior "breezeway" between the front and garden entrances.

Throughout, the beautiful interior millwork becomes a form of superb architectural furnishing, calling for less actual furniture and other wall decorations. One feels a serene sophistication, always fundamental to Means's designs. The heavily molded window surrounds with solid shutters and window seats are particularly decorative, lending simple dignity to Means's 1971 Waldo Moore house.

The owners at the time of this writing, Dr. and Mrs. Michael Clark, knew when they "walked in the door" that this was what they had been looking for. The only changes they made are not apparent from the street. A talented young Georgia architect of the present generation of traditionalists, Keith Summerour, helped them remodel the kitchen and add side garage space. Summerour's work for the Clarks respects Means's classic essay on the eighteenth-century Charleston townhouse mode, as built three decades ago for his friend Dr. Waldo Moore.

Opposite: Front elevation.
Above: Rear detail, showing basement-level door and Palladian window.

LIVING-ROOMS
FAMILY GARDENS
COLEFAX & FOWLER

MOORE-CLARK HOUSE.
Left: Entrance/stair hall with view into living room. Top: Living room. Above: Library.

FLORENCE-AIKEN HOUSE

Means client: Dr. and Mrs. Thomas J. Florence.
Place: Atlanta, Cobb County, Georgia. Completion Date: June 1972.
Current Owner: Mr. and Mrs. James A. Aiken.
Style: Maryland manor, early eighteenth-century Georgian colonial.
Contractor/builder: Dan Brothers, 1972; Paul Koehn,1994.
Millwork: Jim Girdler, W. P. Stephens Lumber Co.
Interim Owners: various developers.
The Houses of James Means, *pp. 22–23.*

Left: Entrance elevation and motor court. Above: View from hall into dining room.

James Means was an inventive classicist; such a statement could seem contradictory. His design for this house is original at the same time that it is classical. His design is a variation on the theme of Maryland manor house, an early- to mid-eighteenth-century Georgian colonial vernacular style. This house has few exact antecedents but many close cousins. It is not the clone or twin of any one house from the Chesapeake Bay area, but it would be at home there.

It is as though a builder-architect for the Maryland plantation aristocracy had come back to life in 1971–72 to build pre-revolutionary Maryland manor in Cobb County, Georgia, for Dr. and Mrs. Thomas J. (Glenna) Florence. Along Maryland's eastern shore the brick house, almost always laid in Flemish bond, as here, had been the ideal. The Florences' house also has the T-shaped plan popular in Maryland and often used by James Means.

One of the most recognizable cousins for this house is Readborne (1732 and later), a two-story brick, early Georgian-style manor in Queen Anne's County. Readborne's arched front door with fan-lighted transom seems to have spawned the Florences', down to the decorative rubbed and gauged vermilion brick arch outlining the rear Palladian motif of the entranceway. In the entrance hall this arched transom overdoor theme is repeated, a familiar Means millwork detail in many variations among his works.

The Florences first met Jimmy Means at a Means restoration, the nearby home of Mary and Sandy Pike. (See page 90.) Also in the area is another Maryland colonial–style adaptation, the Means design for Dr. and Mrs. Walter Bloom. (See page 44.) The Blooms left this part of east Cobb County once it began to grow by proverbial leaps and bounds. So would the Florences. But when their project was begun in 1970 and the area was still somewhat rural, they acquired seventeen acres. The sort of estate they developed seemed appropriate then. They had twin lakes and a gazebo beyond, four outbuildings, and many boxwood in formal patterns.

Two years before building began, Means started taking the Florences around Georgia, educating them by visiting old houses, Dr. Florence has said. He says that Means once told him why they should spend the large amount of

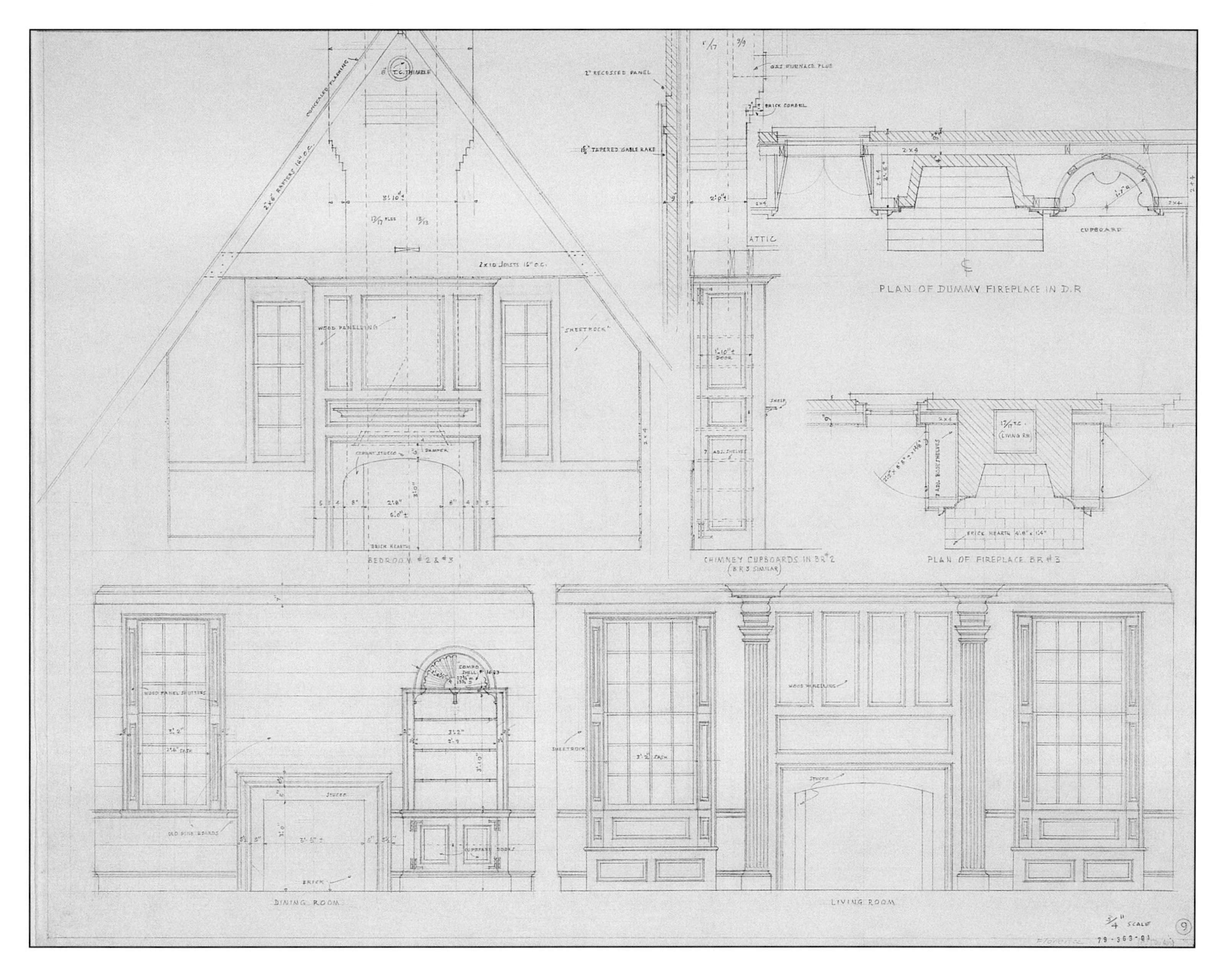

money to pay for the expensive paneling in the entrance hall: "Go on and do it, you'll be happy later on."

The first time the author saw the exterior of the Florence house was after the seventeen acres had been subdivided into a cul-de-sac of numerous brand-new houses of less architectural distinction that this. It was recognizable as one of Jimmy Means's, and it stood out from the others so decidedly, on its little hill, that it was a startling demonstration of "best of show." By that time, however, it had been through hell and back.

Those who brought it back were Mr. and Mrs. James A. Aiken. Mrs. Aiken had known Dr. Florence, and she knew that he and Mrs. Florence had sold the house and acreage to a Cobb County builder, who later went bankrupt. The house, which stood empty for years, at one time was a private preschool facility. The Aikens took over in the spring of 1994.

The Aikens have done a splendid job of restoration, a labor of more than love, of passion, really, to bring it back. It is as if they had become Means's clients and were determined to carry out his design to the letter, again. Their only significant change from the original was to take down a wall in the kitchen to open the area into the kind of family room–kitchen combination much prized in the 1990s. That was a small sacrifice to make for such a large accomplishment, the saving of the Florence house from the further ravages of time. The Florences' Means-designed gazebo was relocated about 1990 to woodland gardens on the grounds of the Atlanta History Center. (See page 15)

Florence-Aiken House.
Opposite page: Living room.
Above: Fireplace wall elevations and details for dining room, living room, and bedrooms two and three.

FORBES-RAYBURN HOUSE

Means client: Mr. Walter Forbes and Mrs. F. D. (Betty Forbes) Rayburn.
Place: Marshallville, Macon County, Georgia. Completion Date: 1972.
Current Owner: Mr. and Mrs. F. D. Rayburn.
Style: Georgia vernacular.
Contractor/builder: Mrs. Rayburn and George Colvin.
The Houses of James Means, *pp. 96–97.*

Marshallville, Macon County, Georgia, is due west of Perry and I-75. On the Norfolk-Southern railroad and near the Flint River flowing through the county, it is peach- and camellia-growing country. Macon County, which had been Creek Indian territory, was created out of two older counties in 1837. One of Marshallville's best-known native sons was John Donald Wade (1892-1963), a descendent of the first settlers of the area, a Columbia University Ph.D. and a Vanderbilt Agrarian writer who, at the University of Georgia in 1947, founded the *Georgia Review*, still a nationally important literary quarterly. Wade returned to Marshallville in the 1950s and became an authority on camellias, a gardener, and a horticulturist.

One of the two James Means restoration-renovations in this Forbes-Rayburn family compound, the one called Dingley Dell, had been an early Wade family place, built in the 1830s. It became Walter Forbes's house. Mrs. Forbes was deceased, but this had been her land, and she was a Wade relative. The other house, Felderfield (two surnames, Felder and Field), dates from the 1840s. It was done for Forbes's daughter, Mrs. F. D. (Betty Forbes) Rayburn. Both houses were moved onto the site, which contains a large lake. The compound is sometimes called Malatchie, a Creek Indian name.

Betty Forbes Rayburn attended Sweet Briar College in Virginia with Margaret Davison Block of Atlanta. Betty has always loved old houses. She asked Margaret (Mrs. Bates) Block to recommend an architect for her and her father's proj-

Felderfield. Top: Side view from lake. Above left: Front elevation. Left: East side and rear. Opposite: Entrance/stair hall.

FORBES-RAYBURN HOUSE. Above: Dingley Dell. Right: Dining room at Felderfield.

ect. James Means was first on the list because moving and restoring old houses was one of his strong suits. (Margaret Block's sister was married to the antique dealer Kenneth Garcia, Sr., a close associate of Means's in the Stone Mountain restoration project.)

Dingley Dell, the Forbes place, is one of the oldest houses in the Marshallville area. One story, painted grey with white trim, it has half-log underpinnings and other features that indicate its early date. The two front rooms are the original living room and bedroom. Means composed the small country neoclassical porch, drew replacement mantels for the missing originals in the front rooms, added a bedroom wing, and connected a small back room to a kitchen with a bay window.

Felderfield, Betty Rayburn's house, is a story-and-a-half, plantation-plain vernacular farmhouse from the 1840s. It stands next to woods in a forty-acre meadow that slopes to the lake. Painted yellow with white trim, it has four equal-sized rooms on the main floor, with board ceilings, wainscoting, and lath and plaster walls. The original doors, flooring, and mantels of heart pine have been restored. The double front doors open to a central hall with a fourteen-foot ceiling, a plan early settlers evolved for the hot middle-Georgia climate.

Means added an open front porch with slender columns from an old house in Athens, Georgia; the bricks for the four Means-designed chimneys also came from Athens. (This house had been built by a Colonel Fudge, who is now the resident ghost, they say, a friendly ghost who is quite welcome.) Means added a lattice screened back porch to which the kitchen is attached; for this quite necessary room, he created an arched corner fireplace and mantel, which is the family's favorite spot.

When Means first came down to the empty site, he said to Betty Rayburn, "Well, what do you want?" They rode around the generous, relatively flat setting to envision Malatchie. It was a place and project made for him. During two years, Means worked closely with Mrs. Rayburn and a local carpenter-builder, George Colvin, a jack-of-all-trades (like Means). Colvin told them that in the 1960s he had helped move an old house in nearby Perry. Colvin was therefore undaunted. Old materials used for restoration came from an 1840s house, the Belvin house in early Houston County records, already on the place. They also took down two derelict houses in Marshallville for their parts. The hearth bricks in the renovated kitchen came from the old Asbury Methodist Church in Marshallville. (*The Houses of James Means* reported, "Country living with the enticement of fried chicken, turnip greens and cornbread brought Mr. Means from Atlanta to oversee work on the project.")

TOON HOUSE

Means client: Mr. and Mrs. Ralph L. Toon, Jr.
Place: Atlanta. Completion Date: June 1972.
Style: Colonial Williamsburg, Virginia.
Contractor/builder: Ralph Toon.
Millwork: Jim Girdler, W. P. Stephens Lumber Co.
The Houses of James Means, *pp. 24–25.*

Means's house for Dr. and Mrs. Florence, in Cobb County, Georgia, was being built at the same time, 1971–72, as the Toons' house in Atlanta in the Peachtree Heights Park section of suburban Buckhead. The two houses were completed in June 1972. Nancy Toon grew up on the established street where they found a lot, she says, which "Jimmy Means didn't like," because he liked for "a house to breathe." He had wanted them to find some land out in the country like the Florences had. Means said he didn't like to design "a Palladian window that had to fight for its life" in a cramped setting.

When Mrs. Toon was twenty-six years old, she passed a house under construction that reminded her of houses she had known in Virginia. Her grandparents' home there had been built in 1850. She decided that she, too, could have a Virginia house. She says, "I am a throwback." She saw Means's Milner house, and she knew some of the people who had used Means as their architect, including the Herbert Wests. (See page 166.) She decided to have Means design and build them "an old house."

They had taken Sunday afternoon rides with Means to see houses he designed, was building, or had once helped with before he was on his own. The Toons felt that it was like "a year in Georgia Tech's School of Architecture." Ralph Toon says, "Means won every battle" in building their house, including coloring the mortar with red clay from their property for their expensive Flemish-bond brickwork of wood-molded Virginia brick. Because Ralph Toon was his own contractor, he worked particularly closely with Means. Toon says jovially that their "millwork cost more than they sold the other house for."

They also went in search of old building materials, finding, for example, some old heart-pine flooring from Greensboro, Georgia, covered in mud when they first saw it. They found additional heart pine that had been in the Georgia Capitol until it was replaced by tile, and more from Atlanta's Kimball house, a post–Civil War hotel destroyed in 1959.

The specific eighteenth-century house at Williamsburg, Virginia, on which they based the entrance façade is known as Blair's Brick House. It and the Toons' house have dormers and a jerkin-head roof. The Wythe house at Williamsburg is the basis of the design of the front hall; this spacious stair hall leads to a large living room on the rear in another one of Means's T-shaped plans. The plan allows for many windows and access to the outside, on the east to a side parterre garden of English boxwood.

Their driveway, lined with a flowering pear tree allée, often saw Jimmy Means arriving "with little sketches" in hand that he wanted to share with his friends and "students," Nancy and Ralph Toon. For this book the Toons have shared some of these, which are shown in the Portfolio. One of them is a diagrammatic study Means did of a two-story Williamsburg house showing the "lineaments," or controlling lines that produced the system of proportion those old Virginia builders-architects used—equilateral triangles and enscribing circles that made their designs so logical and visually satisfying. (See page 21.) A similar study for the George Wythe house is shown in Marcus Whiffen's *The Eighteenth Century Houses of Williamsburg* (1960). Not only was Nancy Toon a throwback, but fortunately so was James Means.

Opposite: Entrance elevation. Above: Entrance/stair hall.

Mrs. Toon was the coordinator for *The Houses of James Means*. In 1978, with Means's approval and cooperation, she had undertaken a Means house tour to benefit the American Cancer Society, because she "wanted to honor Jimmy in his lifetime." That tour grew into the house book, which was published in the fall of 1979 after Means's accidental death. In the process Nancy and Ralph Toon became even greater Means experts than they already were as a result of having worked with him to create their house, where they still reside after some thirty years. The first people interviewed for the present book were Ralph and Nancy Toon, in October 1998.

For Southern Architecture Foundation, in March 2000 Nancy and Ralph Toon hosted a James Means evening about this book. We met in the big high-ceilinged living room of their historic T-shaped house. The Toons continue to honor their architect-friend for what he helped them achieve a generation ago.

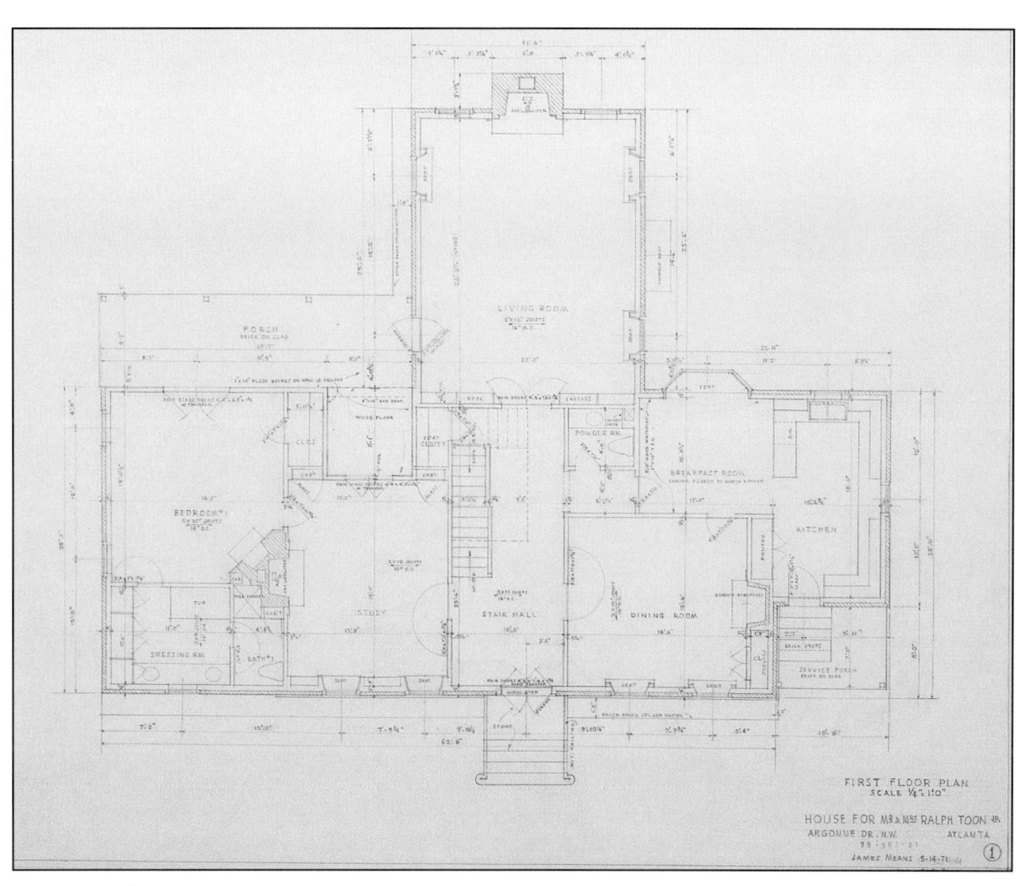

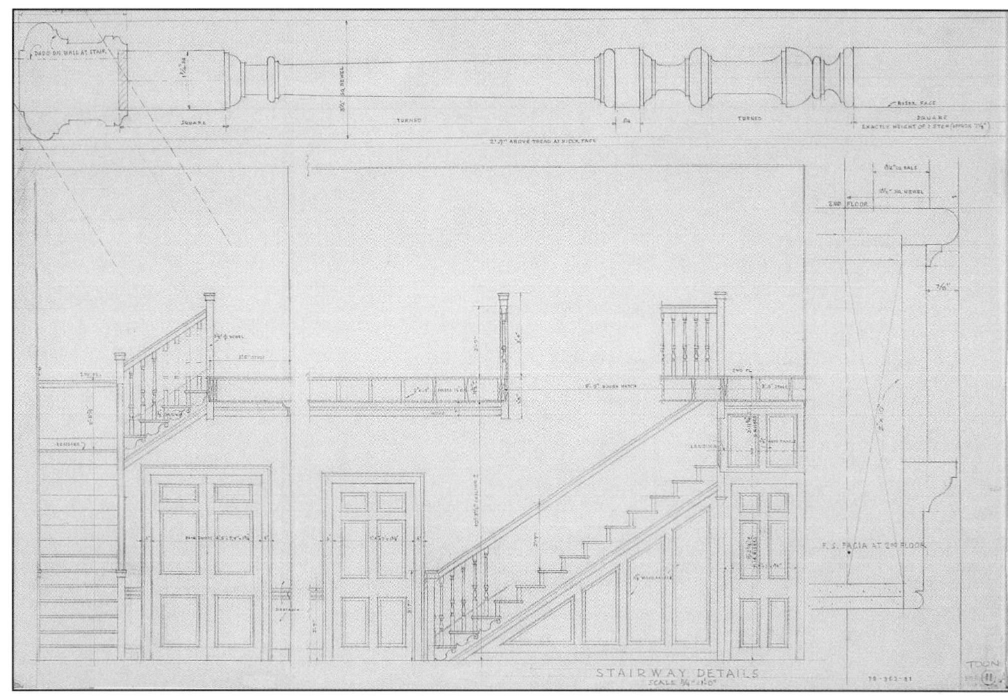

TOON HOUSE.
Left: Dining room. Top: First floor plan. Above: Stairway details.

COXE-NUNNALLY HOUSE

Means client: Mr. and Mrs. Tench Coxe.
Place: Atlanta. Completion Date: November 1974.
Current Owner: Mr. and Mrs. C. Talbot Nunnally III.
Style: French provincial farmhouse.
Contractor/builder: Byron Parker.
Millwork: Jim Girdler, W. P. Stephens Lumber Co.
The Houses of James Means, *pp. 86–87.*

The versatility and eclectic inventiveness of James Means is well illustrated by the preceding middle Georgia farmhouses and this house, described as a French farmhouse in *The Houses of James Means*. In that 1979 book, this house is headlined "A French House in Atlanta," and the data describe it as an eighteen-month project completed in November 1974. Means's drawings for this French farmhouse are dated June 13, 1973, eighteen months before, just as the houses book reported.

In the November 1986 issue of *House Beautiful* magazine, this house was featured as "American Spirit, French Style," in a ten-page interior decorating spread. Again, as in the Means tribute book, the owners were not identified. However, a *Southern Accents* article in spring 1981 identified the Means clients as Frankie and Tench Coxe. That was a garden story, "An Enchanting Garden Secluded Behind Stucco Walls," and James Means was given deserved credit for the garden design under the title at the top of the article.

House Beautiful reported, "James Means, who had built many distinguished houses, was most famous for his early American structures and restorations." Without attribution, Frankie Coxe was quoted, "Although he had designed fewer French houses, we wanted Jimmy Means because his sense of proportion was so wonderful." Coxe was a "confirmed Francophile," the magazine said. "When he showed us photographs of a house in Vézelay [from the *Tuilleries Brochures*, 1932] we told him it was exactly what we want, with all the openness and light you get in a contemporary house." Mrs. Coxe certainly understood Means, because she told that writer, "We didn't want a copy of an old house, but the feeling of one."

Not in the countryside, but just off West Wesley Road in the northwest Atlanta suburbs, the Coxe house sits on a hillside lot carefully landscaped to give a sense of walled, domestic privacy. The owners wanted a "big-little town-

Opposite: Front entrance from motor court. Above: Rear (garden) view. Below: Living room.

house-farmhouse," as it was described in the houses book.

It resembles a small manor (*manoir*) with mansard roof, creamy stucco, large casement windows and casement doors with batten-board shutters. A series of these tall French doors with arched transoms opens onto the side walled terrace and formal garden with a chinoiserie gazebo built of timbers from an old house in Elberton, Georgia. The house and garden merge into unified living spaces, walled in and private.

The interior is also a design of merging spaces: living room, dining room paved with terra cotta, kitchen, and stairway, all unified with arched openings over doors and windows. Beams in the dining room ceiling and the flooring in the living room came from the same house as the old timbers in the gazebo. One enters from a paved courtyard with minimal planting. This is restrained French taste as interpreted by a Georgia architect who knew a thing or two about farmhouse functionalism, wherever it might be found.

Mr. and Mrs. Talbot (Jill) Nunnally III couldn't resist it, and in 1998 another Means house found its ideal owners. The photographs show that this young couple have found the perfect French farmhouse in suburban Atlanta in which to raise a brood of children. Such a house should help them with their French.

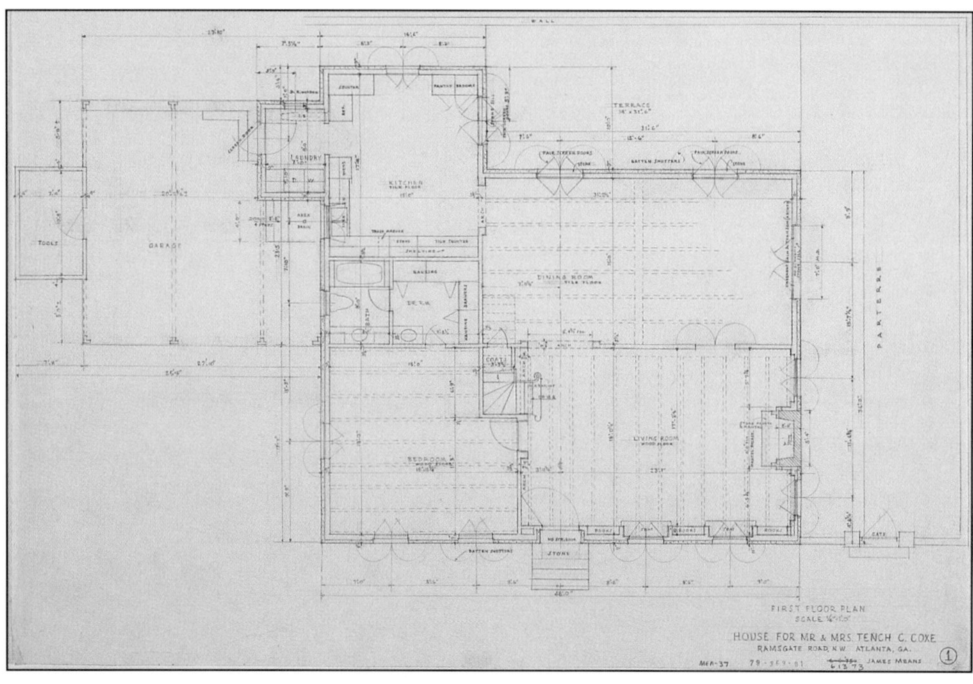

COXE-NUNNALLY HOUSE.
Above: Living room. Left: First floor plan.
Opposite: View of stairs and dining room from living room.

KENNEDY HOUSE

Means client: Mr. and Mrs. Alfred D. Kennedy.
Place: Atlanta. Completion Date: October 1974.
Style: Palladian Italianate.
Contractor/builder: Cecil Malone Construction Co.
Millwork: Jim Girdler, W. P. Stephens Lumber Co.
The Houses of James Means, *pp. 88–89.*

In late 1974 James Means was busy finishing two other Atlanta projects based on European styles. In October he completed this Italianate villa, Palladian in character, that he had begun three years before for Alfred D. Kennedy (1916–1983) and Mrs. Kennedy (Virginia Hightower), who still resides here.

The Kennedys' house recalls Means's days with Hentz, Reid & Adler, when he was architect Neel Reid's hands in the 1920s, when the firm did such designs as the Andrew Calhoun house and the Joseph Rhodes house. That was the time of the Florida boom, when Spanish-tile roofs and baroque arches for a short while became the fashion in suburban Buckhead. Means did seven French houses, but this is his only house in an Italian style.

Villa Serenità is the name the Kennedys gave their three-story Italianate home. They built on part of a Kennedy family tract out from town on a ridge above the Chattahoochee River. At first they thought of building one of Means's Georgia farmhouses, but their architect, who highly approved of the site, advised them that their beautiful continental furnishings called for something a bit more sophisticated. Means said, "Can you see this furniture in a 'farmhouse'?"

During the long building process the couple took their plans to Vicenza, Italy (home of things Palladian). They purchased columns, keystones, chimney caps, statues, mantels, and other lavastone pieces that Means specified. Everything fit perfectly.

The yellow stucco exterior is somewhat more baroque than pure Palladian, which is reflected in the interior architecture and in the interior decoration. A well-known Atlanta interior decorator who helped Mrs. Kennedy, the late Edith Hills, was famous for her highly stylish, perhaps a bit theatri-

Left: Entrance elevation. Below left: Detail of front entrance. Below right: Niche on exterior of greenhouse wall. Above: Entrance hall.

cal, continental taste. "Rococola" is a word the writer John Dos Passos (1896–1970) coined to describe Atlanta during the Jazz Age—a rollicking pun combining rococo and Coca-Cola, the town's richest product. Edith Hills would probably have liked the idea. Dos Passos, of course, was writing about the Neel Reid era. But if there were such a style as Rococola, then Villa Serenità, by James Means and the Kennedys, should be seen as its revival—and copyrighted like Coca-Cola's secret formula.

The late Alfred Kennedy was one of the greatest patrons of grand opera in Atlanta. Perhaps Villa Serenità was his way of reminding people of the eternal beauty of the classics, of the importance of classical art and architecture, no matter the era.

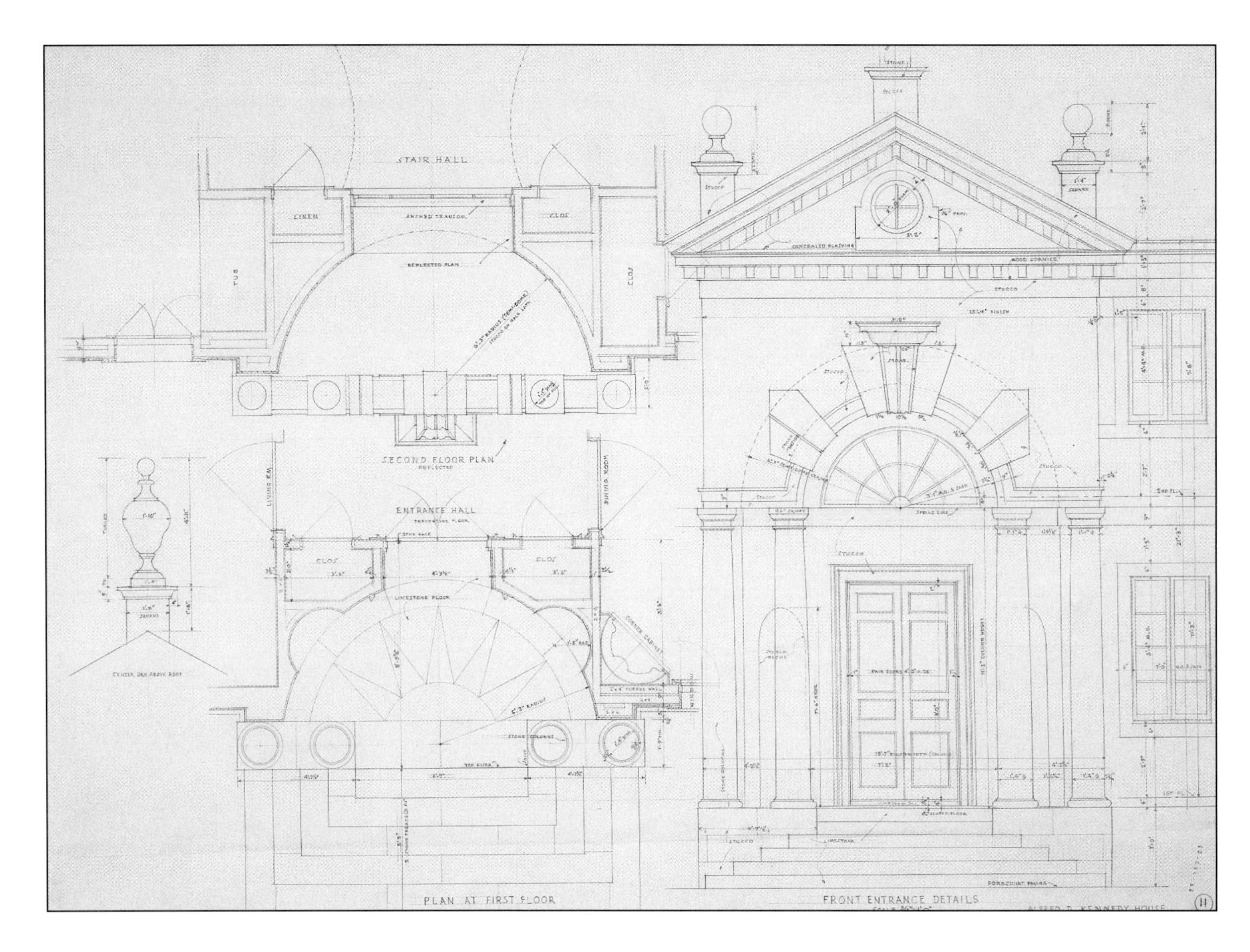

STAIR HALL
SECOND FLOOR PLAN
ENTRANCE HALL
PLAN AT FIRST FLOOR
FRONT ENTRANCE DETAILS

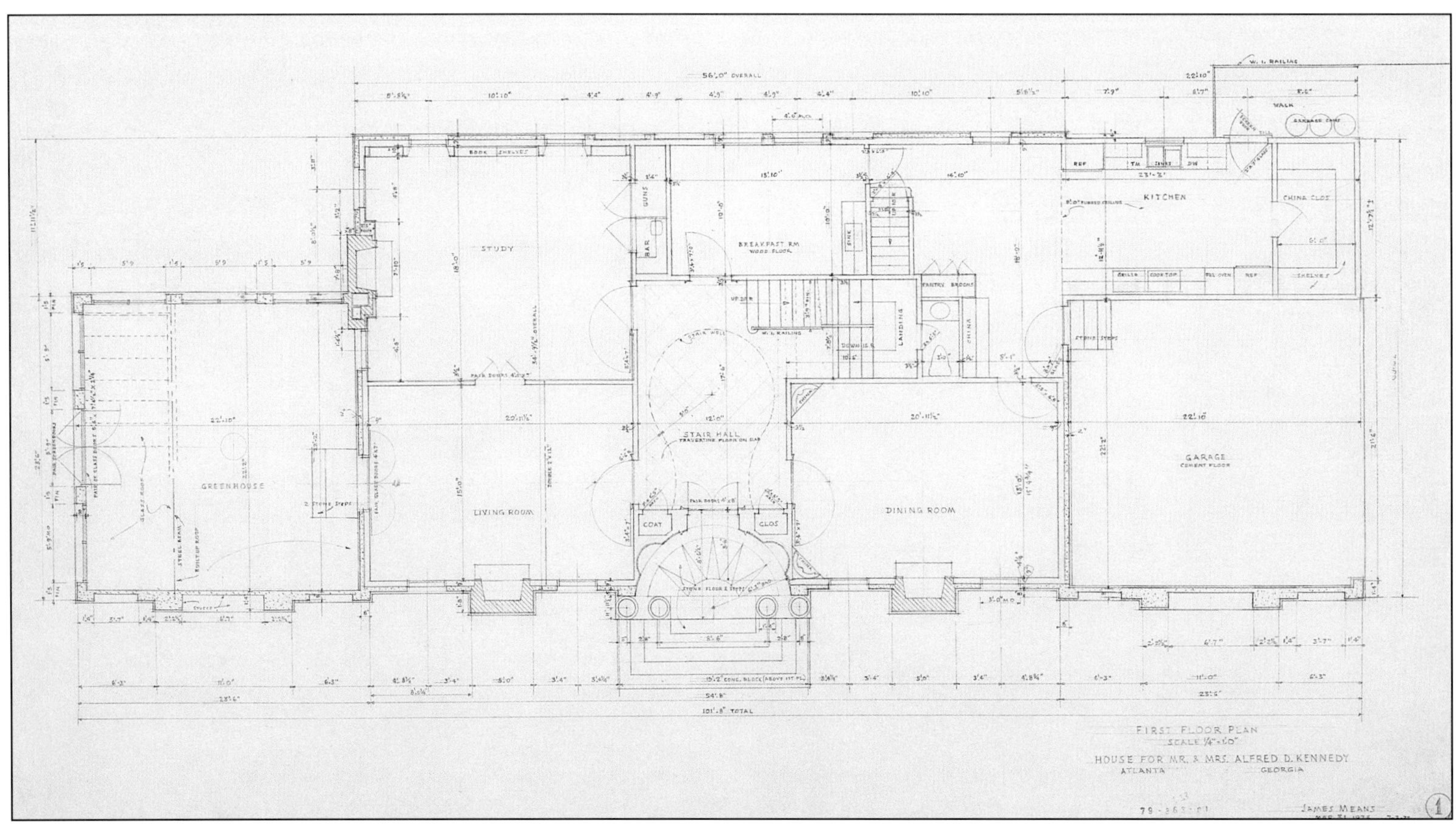

STUDY
BREAKFAST RM
KITCHEN
GREENHOUSE
LIVING ROOM
STAIR HALL
DINING ROOM
GARAGE
FIRST FLOOR PLAN
HOUSE FOR MR. & MRS. ALFRED D. KENNEDY
ATLANTA GEORGIA
JAMES MEANS

Kennedy House.
Opposite top: Plan of hall and front entrance details.
Opposite bottom: First floor plan.
Above: Study with view into living room.
Right. Living room.

KLEINER-KNOX HOUSE

Means client: Dr. Jack Kleiner.
Place: Atlanta. Completion Date: 1972–73.
Current Owner: Mr. and Mrs. Larry Knox.
Style: Colonial Philadelphia; Queen Anne/early Georgian.
Later architect: Norman Davenport Askins.
Interim Owners: Dr. and Mrs. William E. Huger, Jr.
Not included in The Houses of James Means

Below: Entrance elevation.
Opposite top: Living room.
Opposite bottom: Stair hall.

The Means plans for this house for Dr. Jack Kleiner are dated December 12, 1972. Kleiner was a Georgia Tech engineering professor. This project was not included in *The Houses of James Means*, because the architect and the engineer disagreed about budget and details; the last straw, evidently, was about exactly how the bricks were being laid, in Flemish bond, and about the mortar joint. One person who lived in the house after Dr. Kleiner said, "They divorced each other" before the house was entirely completed.

That was not the only time that Means and a client parted company over a project. Even so, Means was the designer, even if he was much peeved about how his plans were being carried out in the final building stages. However, the house has been owned, appreciated, and sold as a "Jimmy Means house."

The second owners, Dr. and Mrs. William E. Huger, Jr., bought it because of the Means connection. An odd sidelight is that Dr. Huger's sister, Mrs. J. Ray (Callie Huger) Efird, was editor and designer of *The Houses of James Means*. William E. (Billy) Huger III, the Hugers' son, a Southern Architecture Foundation board member, grew up here. His mother, Trudy Munns Huger, Dr. Huger's widow, sold it to Larry and Paula Knox in 1994. The Hugers had had Atlanta classicist Norman Askins do some work on the house for them.

The Knoxes, in turn, employed Askins to help make restorations and renovations when they became the owners. With the help of Askins, among other things the Knoxes accomplished was the restoration of the little front porch entranceway, adding new millwork to replicate rotted elements, and renewing the stucco on the hood. That improvement is the only change apparent from the street.

The Knoxes had looked at numerous Means houses, hoping to buy one of them as their own. They were looking for a larger house in which to raise their three children. They considered the Efird and the Milner houses, and they admired the Hennessy house. The Knoxes saw the potential, the "good bones," of the Kleiner house, Paula Knox said.

Means's Kleiner design partakes of the spirit of early eighteenth-century colonial Queen Anne–period Philadelphia. (Stenton, c. 1728, at Germantown, comes to mind.) It is an austere beauty that depends on geometry and symmetry, and by Flemish bond brickwork highlighted by a string course marking the second floor and by jack arches at the windows, all of it accentuated by small rubbed and gauged bricks brighter in hue than the bond.

Sited on two acres on a slight rise behind a long sweep of meadow and lawn, far back from a suburban northwest Atlanta road, its broad horizontality quietly dominates the long landscape. It suggests a colonial college or school building; perhaps Dr. Kleiner's profession influenced the architect's design.

ROOKER-WARREN HOUSE

Means client: Mr. and Mrs. William A. Rooker, Jr.
Place: Atlanta (Cobb County). Completion Date: September 1974.
Current Owner: Mr. and Mrs. James K. Warren.
Style: Eighteenth-century French provincial.
Contractor/builder: Byron Parker; Brad Hodges for the Warrens.
Millwork: Jim Girdler, W. P. Stephens Lumber Co.
Interim Owners: Mr. and Mrs. Don Sentell.
The Houses of James Means, *pp. 84–85.*

In the late summer of 1974 two James Means houses, both French in style, were being completed, the preceding Tench Coxe and this, the William Rooker, which was the larger of the two. In Means's own terminology the Rooker house has quite enough land around it to be able to "breathe." Its considerable privacy comes not from walled gardens and other formal landscape features but from the seclusion the surrounding acreage provides. Means liked for his clients to have at least one creek; the Rooker house has a river. This is the fifth of the Means French houses, following his first in 1956 for Arthur Montgomery. The seventh and last is the Anderberg-Huff, discussed in the conclusion.

Located on a wooded twenty-five-acre estate on the Chattahoochee River in the Vinings area of Cobb County, Georgia, the Rooker house is approached by a winding drive through a naturalistic landscape. There are glimpses on the east of white-water rapids. The mansard roof of the two-story cream stucco French provincial *manoir* comes into view as one enters a gravel forecourt bordered by cobblestones. Once inside the entrance stair hall, panoramic views of the landscaped flood plain begin to be seen below in the distance. These outside views are part of every room on the riverside, from French doors opening onto a deep terrace.

Since its completion, this estate has been home to only three families. First credit for its creation goes to Mr. and Mrs. William A. (Mary Scott) Rooker, who assembled the property and an experienced group of experts. James (Jimmy) Means led the team that included landscape architect William (Billy) Monroe (1927–99), builder Byron Parker, and millwork specialist Jim Girdler.

The present owners, Rebekah and James (Jimmy) Warren, a young couple with deep Atlanta roots, purchased their private hideaway in August 1996. Warren found the house in April 1996 through his builder, Brad Hodges, when it was owned by Mr. and Mrs. Don Sentell. Jimmy Warren was looking for land on which to build a home for Rebekah. He read a real-estate flyer about the house, which mentioned James Means and William Monroe, whom he already knew because Mrs. Monroe is a cousin of his father. He set out to learn more

about Means, asking his parents and Bill Rooker. They quickly enlightened him. Rooker said working with Jimmy Means, especially searching out old building materials throughout Georgia, was "a fabulous experience."

After the Warrens acquired the property they added solid French exterior shutters to the house, exactly as shown on the original working drawings. The young couple considers a major aspect of the value of their house to be the way it was created with the help of James Means and other experts. Whenever they make necessary modifications for rearing their family here, they intend to preserve the classic beauty of the place to which they have fallen heirs.

James Warren is a founding director and officer of Southern Architecture Foundation. In November 1998, here at their Means-designed home, Jimmy and Rebekah Warren hosted the inaugural fundraiser for the foundation's first publishing project, *The Architecture of James Means*.

Opposite: Front elevation. Top: Rear elevation. Left: View toward house from Chattahoochee River plain. Above: View from house toward river.

Rooker-Warren House.
Left: Living room. Above: Dining room.

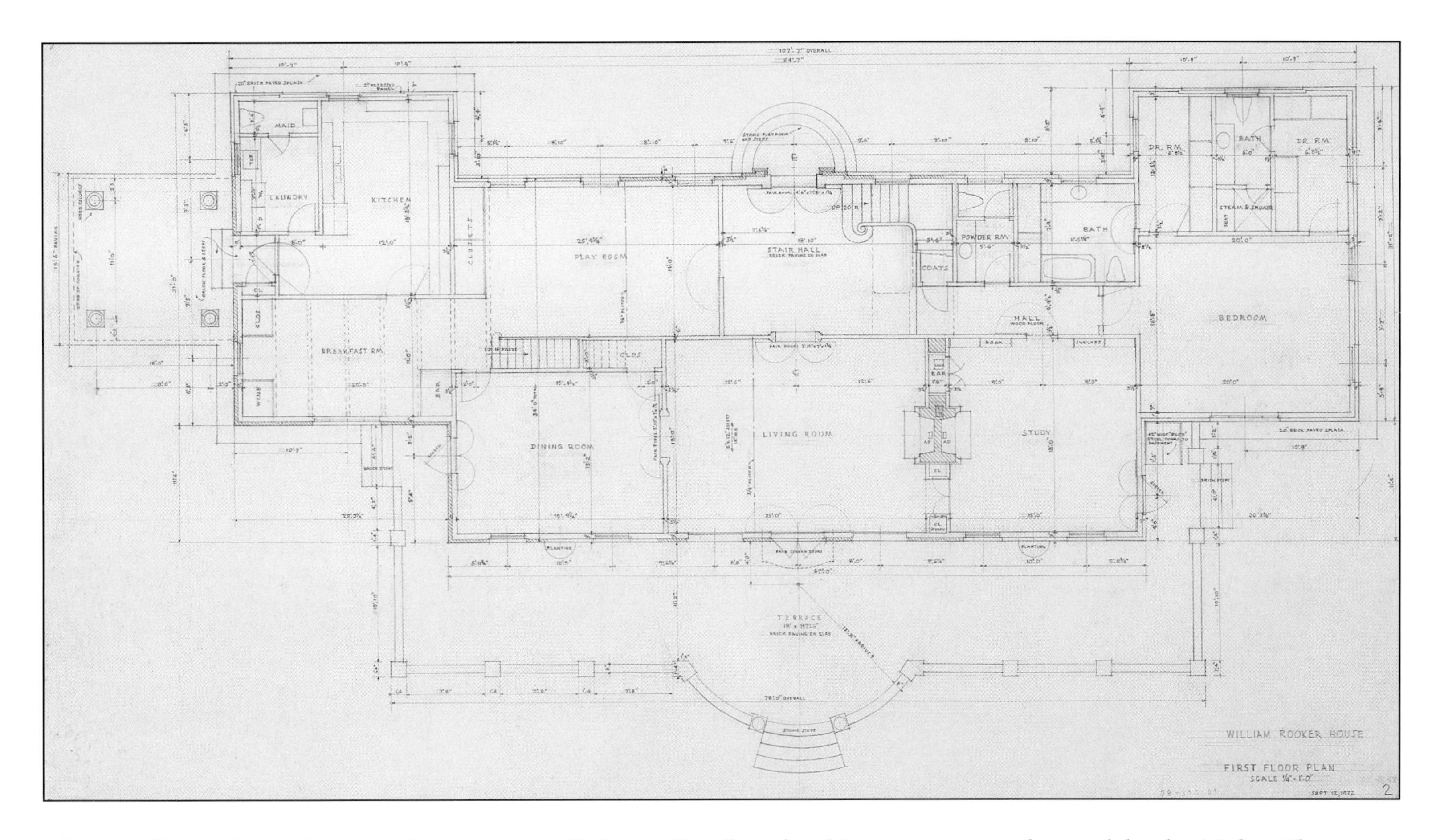

ROOKER-WARREN HOUSE. Opposite: Entrance/stair hall. Above: First floor plan. (Note entrance is at the top of the plan.) Below: Playroom.

HENNESSY HOUSE

Means client: Mr. and Mrs. Robert D. Hennessy.
Place: Atlanta. Completion Date: June 1975.
Style: American Georgian, late eighteenth-century period.
Contractor/builder: Byron Parker.
Millwork: Jim Girdler, W. P. Stephens Lumber Co.
The Houses of James Means, *pp. 62–63.*

This American Georgian–style house was completed after eighteen months of construction, in June 1975, for Mr. and Mrs. Robert D. Hennessy. It stood on a long-established street in the Tuxedo Park section of the northwest Atlanta suburbs. Most of the neighborhood was built in the 1920s and '30s; many of the houses were designed by Hentz, Adler & Shutze, the name of the firm with which Means was associated for many years after the death of his mentor, Neel Reid. To the settled street Means added this house, set well back as are the others, but it seems to dominate in a gentle sort of way. It stands out on its large, country-house sweep of lawn, giving even more dignity to what is acknowledged as an exceptional collection of domestic architecture from the pre–World War II classic eclectic period.

Means based his design on the Georgian period in America of the mid to late eighteenth century. The result is reminiscent of works in Virginia and Maryland where Thomas Jefferson's personal form of Palladianism was felt in a series of mansion houses in which the central block, containing the staircase, was served by low wings, flanking dependencies, balanced at either side.

These symmetrical brick houses are sometimes said to have Palladian five-part plans. Architectural historian T. T. Waterman called them "pavilion-type mansions." The rear elevation of the Hennessy house particularly shows this tendency toward subdivision into smaller-scale units. The redbrick with white trim is also Jeffersonian. Another influence was the Hammond-Harwood house in Annapolis, Maryland, 1773–74, by William Buckland, the joiner-architect. It, too, is in five parts and has a central pediment and a pedimented doorway with a fanlight.

Built of pink-red brick laid in Flemish bond, the Hennessy house is another Means project with old pine floor, doors, and paneling. The library paneling is especially handsome; the large keystone motif with volute bracket, repeated in several places inside and outside, appears here too. This graceful ornamental punctuation ties the entire composition together into a harmonious whole.

Mrs. Hennessy told this writer in the summer of 1999 that she had been in her home for twenty-three years. She said that Jimmy Means had built houses for numerous friends. After she met him, she and her late husband, Bob Hennessy, liked him because he was reserved and listened well. She told Means she wanted "lots and lots of closets and large bathroom-dressing rooms." She wanted an open plan, yet somewhat formal too. The plan of the first floor is the reverse of the Milner-Candler house (page 114). Both houses have generous entrance halls with the staircase in a rear L.

James Means had studied the books available to the architect-builders of the early South, such as William Halfpenny's *New and Complete System of Architecture* (1749) and Robert Morris's *Select Architecture* (1757), one of Jefferson's favorite

Opposite: Front entrance. Above: Front elevation from lawn. Below: Rear (garden) view.

books, as well as eighteenth-century editions of Palladio's *Four Books of Architecture*. He also knew firsthand the South's landmark houses. One of those not already mentioned that might have influenced his design of the Hennessy house was Montpelier, the Snowden house,in Prince George's County, from about 1780. It is another of the pedimented, five-part Palladian mansions built of brick, laid in Flemish bond, with rubbed and gauged jack arches over each window.

The Houses of James Means categorized the Robert Hennessy house as Philadelphia Georgian. The style of this house is difficult to pinpoint because Means synthesized many Georgian precedents. We have mentioned some of the influences on his design; perhaps there is a bit of Philadelphia subtly mixed in there, too.

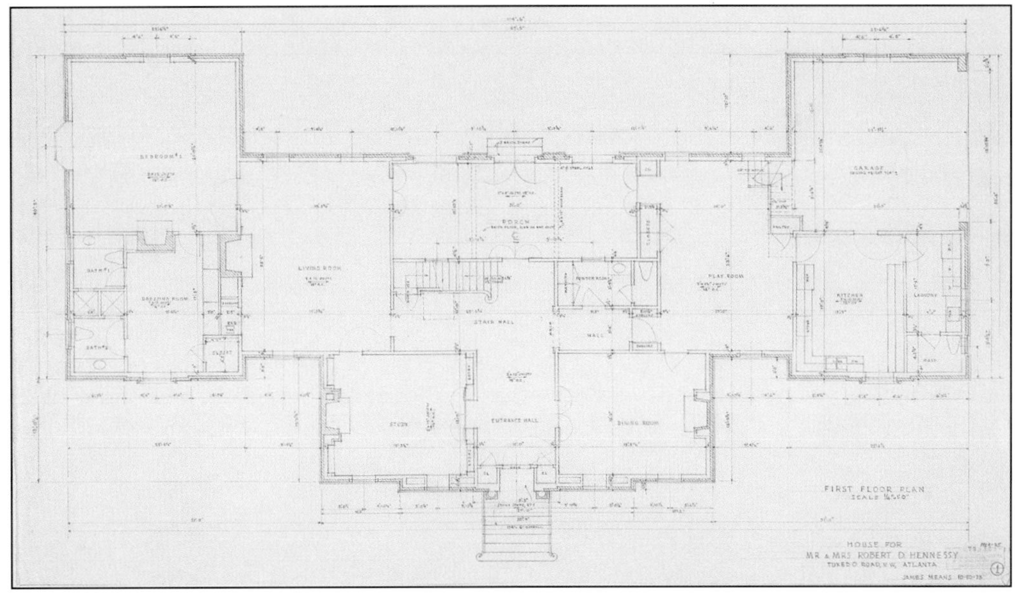

HENNESSY HOUSE.
Left: Stair hall with view into porch. Top: Study with view into living room.
Above: First floor plan.

CAVENDER HOUSE

Means client: Mr. and Mrs. Ralph Cavender.
Place: Claxton, Georgia, vicinity. Completion Date: June 1976.
Style: Eighteenth-century Pennsylvanian.
Contractor/builder: Aubrey Glisson and J. H. Waters, carpenter-builders.
Millwork: Jim Girdler, W. P. Stephens Lumber Co.
The Houses of James Means, *pp. 64–65.*

Because of its deep south Georgia rural setting in Claxton, fifty-five miles due west of Savannah, the eighteenth-century Pennsylvania-style Ralph Cavender house is even more striking from its allée of live oaks than if it were north of the Mason-Dixon line. Means described this two-story T-shaped brick house as having been modeled on such houses as Stenton, 1728, at Germantown. It has a four-square Quaker quality of peaceful, earthly perfection. Made of wood-molded brick, laid in English bond below the water table and Flemish above, it is essentially unadorned outside. Its beauty comes from subtle variations in brick color and symmetrical geometry.

The Cavender house stands out in the flat terrain of southeast Georgia; at the same time its austere perfection seems to reflect the monochromatic, sandy setting. There are twenty-six acres with a pond, lake, smokehouse, an apple orchard, and several formal gardens. Means's design for the total landscape is dated September 1977. That part of the design was an ongoing project, not entirely executed at Means's death.

Ralph Cavender first met in Atlanta with Means, who took him to see the William Parker and Ralph Toon houses there. Later they went to Cobb County to visit the Walter Blooms' place, somewhat similar in style to what Means would design for Cavender, who had to convince Means to take on his project 200 miles from Atlanta. Means went to Claxton every two weeks to supervise, catching a ride with a friend who happened to come on that schedule to a nearby town. Cavender had already been accumulating old building materials from three old houses and other kinds of buildings, slate from a college building at Athens, and heart-pine flooring from a freight depot in Savannah. Means drew for a year before they started building in the winter of 1974. Cavender moved into the house in June 1976. He had already begun planting the live oaks and other trees on the rural site.

Opposite: Entrance elevation. Bottom: Landscape layout.
Left: Garden entrance. Below: Den.

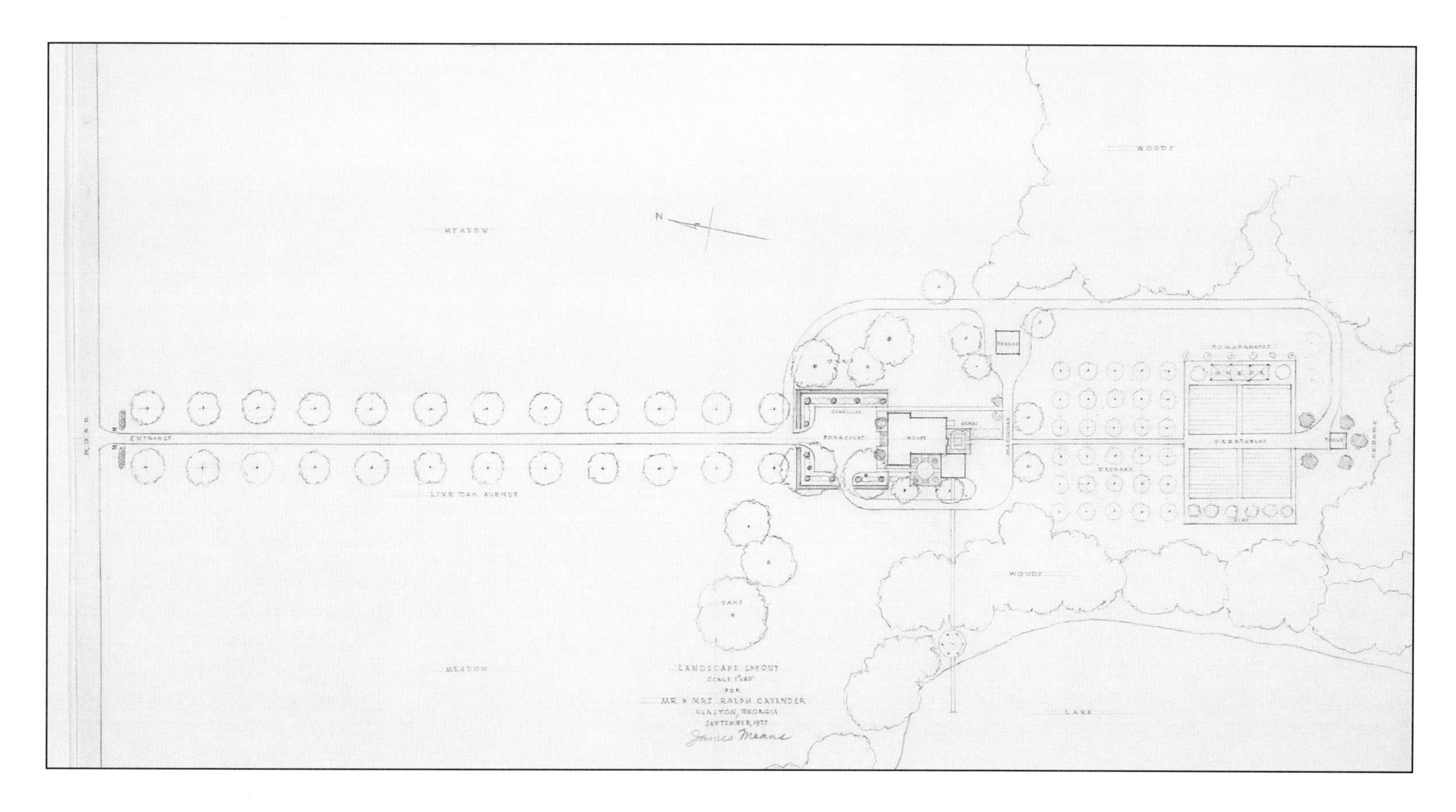

Locally Cavender found two old-time carpenter-builders and a brick mason, patient workers whom he paid by the hour. At first Means was skeptical of these workmen, but he learned to respect their skills and great attitude. The results are evident. The interior architecture has a plainness inspired by the exterior simplicity, its country setting, and early-eighteenth-century Pennsylvanian style.

Means's favorite millwork specialist, Jim Girdler of W. P. Stephens Lumber Company, himself an artist, was involved as he had been with a large percentage of the Means houses. Means said to Cavender about the fanlight on the west entrance of the T from the garden into the study: "You are going to have that fancy fanlight, even if I have to pay Girdler to do it myself!"

Cavender House.
Above: Living room. Right: Master bedroom.
Opposite: Breakfast room and service stair.

PARKER-PARKER HOUSE

Means client: Mr. and Mrs. F. Bowers Parker.
Place: Scottsboro, Alabama, vicinity.
Completion Date: December 1976.
Current Owner: Mr and Mrs. F. Bowers (Bo) Parker, Jr. (son and wife).
Style: Colonial Virginia Palladian.
Contractor/builder: James Michaels; J. H. Devers, brick mason.
Not included in The Houses of James Means.

Above: Front elevation.
Opposite: Brick "cornerstones" in the garage.

This previously unpublished Means house, with its spacious acreage on the outskirts of Scottsboro, Alabama, was not in *The Houses of James Means*. At the time, Means clients Sarah Robinson and Bowers Parker declined to be included, though in later years they expressed regret about their decision. That book had come in 1979, only three years after the completion of this house.

Almost a quarter century later, and proud of the Means-designed home he inherited, Bowers (Bo) Parker, Jr., wanted to share it this time to honor the memory of his parents and that of their architect. The Parkers have opened its handsome front door, welcoming us with pleasure. This is a Southern house in style, and the Parkers' hospitality is greatly appreciated.

Scottsboro is in north Alabama, between Huntsville and the Tennessee River. Means designed a Southern American country house based on plantation prototypes from the Geor-

gian period when a series of Palladian-influenced houses was erected in Tidewater Virginia and Maryland. Among those in Virginia were Mount Airy, Blandford, and Brandon, three brick precedents with flanking two-story connecting dependencies of the kind Means built for the Parkers. The front doorway is also colonial Virginian, a simple version of the garden or south frontispiece of Westover, which was itself based on a precedent from an engraving in William Salmon's style book, *Palladio Londinensis* (1734).

The first date on the Parkers' plan was May 1975. At that time Means was completing the (preceding) Hennessy house in Atlanta, which is somewhat similar in style, being colonial Georgian with a Palladian influence in the five-part layout. The brickwork with both of these houses is beautifully laid Flemish bond, accented with pink rubbed and gauged bricks, like those at Westover. The Ralph Cavender house at Claxton, Georgia, also completed in 1976, enjoys this same kind of glorious brickwork, as does the Alfred Holloway house at Thomaston, Georgia, from 1977.

In the garage of the Parker house is a sort of cornerstone. Incised on four bricks, arranged in vertical order, are the names of the people most directly responsible for the creation of this fine home. The original owners are on the top brick, indicated with their initials, FBP and SRP, and the date, 1976; just below is Jas Means Architect; next Jas Michaels Builder; and then, supporting the rest, comes J. H. Devers Mason. Mr. Devers's brickwork on the tall chimneys at the outside ends of the hipped roof is especially praiseworthy, well deserving of posterity's lasting recognition. The interior central stair hall plan and the millwork, as with all the Means houses, handsomely complements the exterior style and craftsmanship.

We are indebted to the current Parker residents for sharing yet another unpublished example of the domestic architecture of James Means.

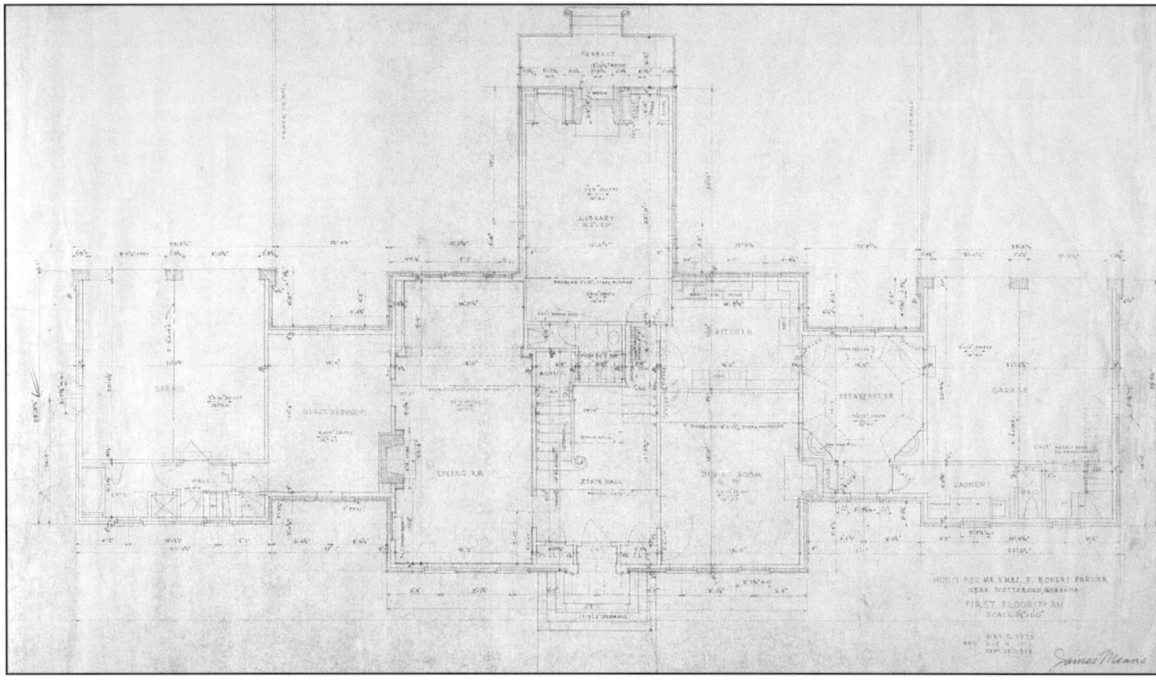

PARKER-PARKER HOUSE.
Above: Living room.
Left: First floor plan.
Opposite: Entrance/stair hall.

KAWAI

Above: Entrance elevation and motor court from garden.
Opposite: Entrance/stair hall.

HOLLOWAY HOUSE

Means client: Dr. and Mrs. Alfred M. Holloway.
Place: Thomaston, Georgia. Completion Date: September 1977.
Style: Colonial Williamsburg.
Contractor/builder: Dr. Holloway.
The Houses of James Means, *pp. 44–45.*

Soon after Barbara and Dr. Al Holloway first met Jimmy Means, their mantra became, "What would Mr. Means think?" They honored him enduringly with "James Means, Architect" incised on an exterior brick.

Means was recommended to them by Grace and Julian Hightower, whose great house at Thomaston, Upson County, Georgia, had been designed in 1948–49 by Philip Shutze (1890–1982), the architect with whom Means was associated for many years, including for the building of their house. Mrs. Hightower believed that Means had been crucial to Shutze's practice and

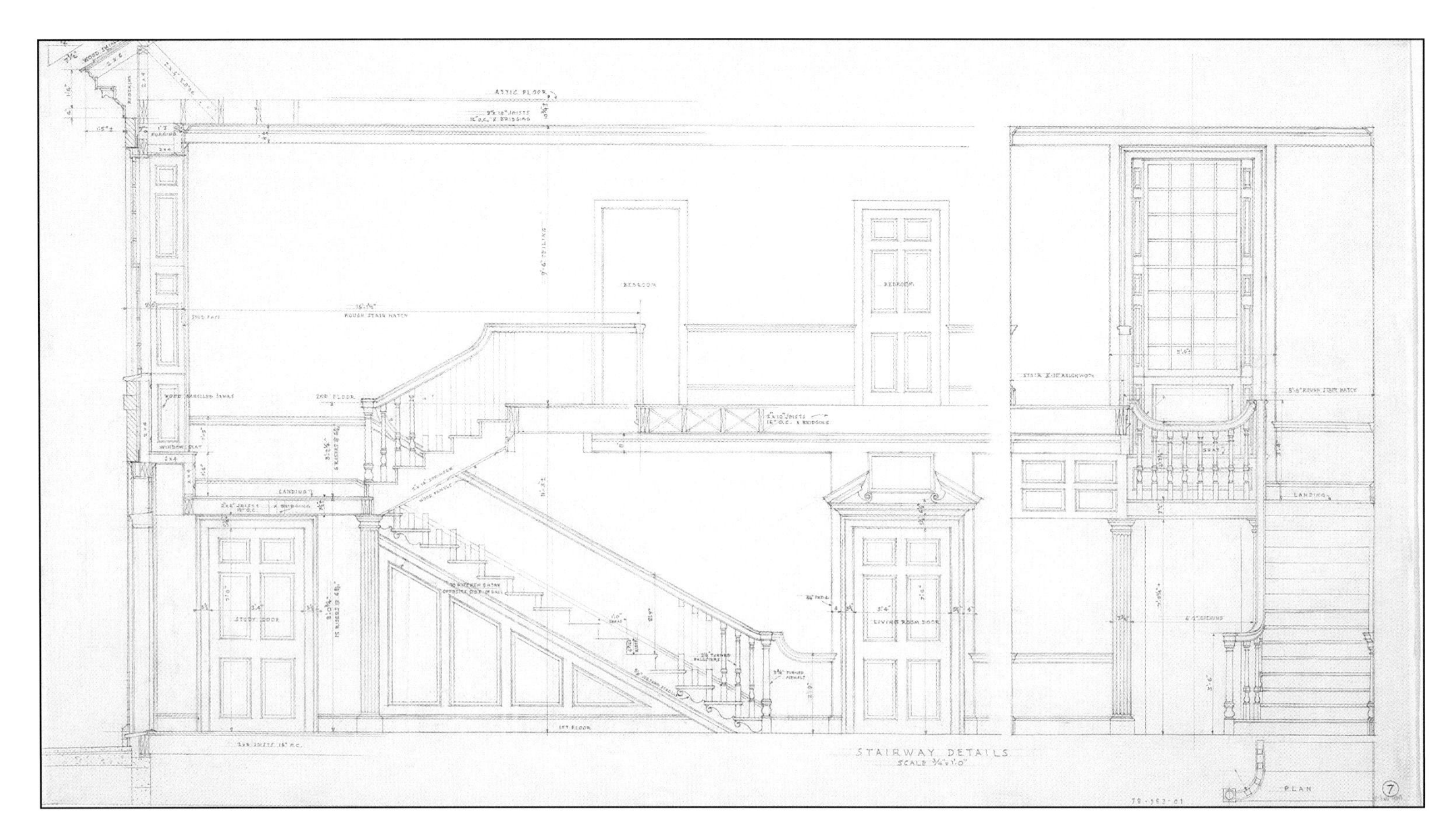

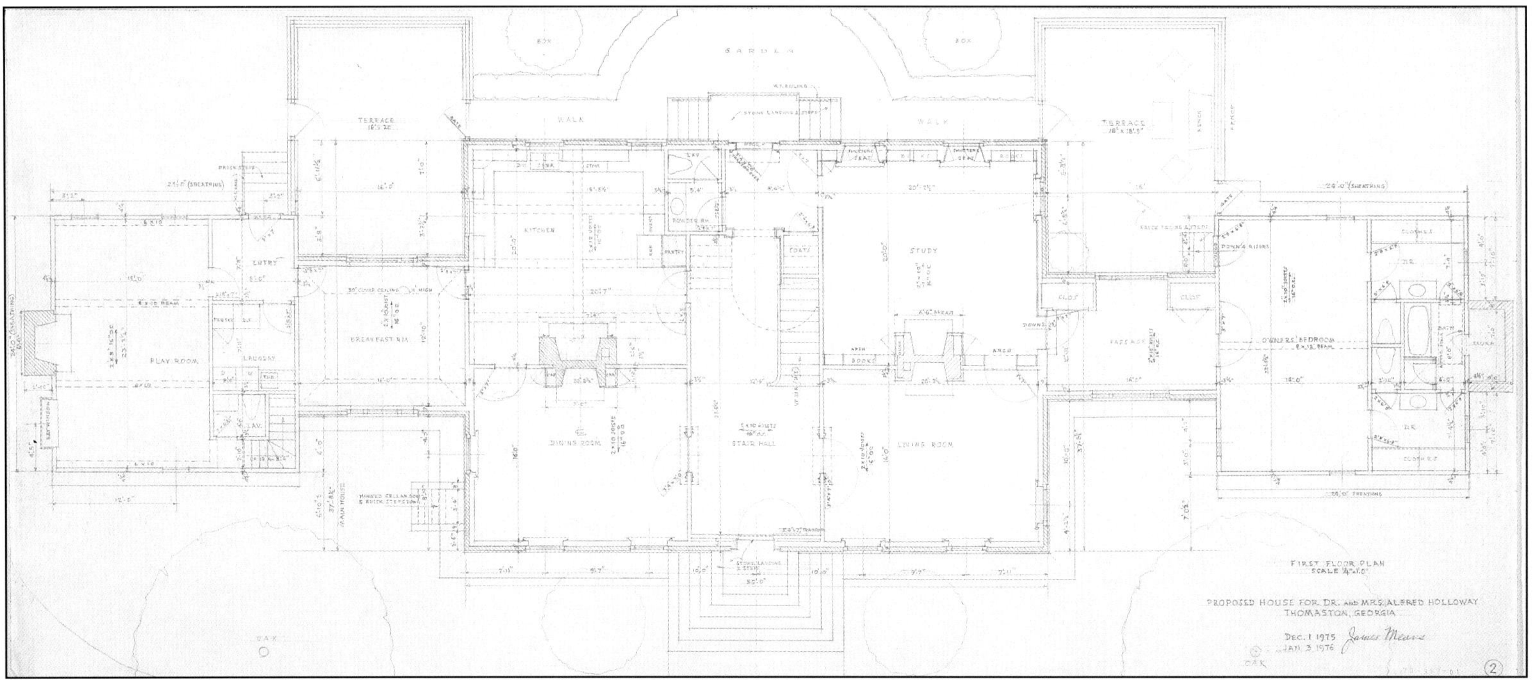

Holloway House.
Top: Stairway details.
Above: First floor plan.
Opposite: Living room.

was his successor. From the Hightowers the Holloways had purchased sixteen acres of land closer to town than the Hightower place, with a perfect hilltop building site looking westward toward the Pine Mountain area in the far distance.

Holly Hill is the Holloways' and Means's version of the restored George Wythe house (c. 1755) at Williamsburg, Virginia, but with the addition of brick hyphens and frame dependencies. Appropriately, the hyphens have Palladian windows, for this is another of Means's five-part Palladian compositions. As with the preceding Cavender house, a serene, geometric beauty results from the Flemish-bond brickwork accented by a bright red string course and, at the windows, jack arches made of rubbed and gauged bricks. It is the Williamsburg style, severe but visually appealing because, in its own mid-eighteenth-century way, it is "streamlined," a no-nonsense, functional directness, that was Means's own personal trademark style, in person and in his designs.

The Holloways originally arranged to meet Means in a Sears-Roebuck parking lot in Atlanta's Buckhead. He was driving "the plainest white car that you could imagine," Barbara Holloway has often said. Means toured them around to see some of his Atlanta houses. When Means went to Thomaston to see their building site, he immediately recommended exactly what he later designed and built. He decided then and there that the setting needed the broad horizontality of the connectors and dependencies attached to a main block patterned after the Wythe house, with its low-pitched hip roof punctuated by the tall verticals of bold chimneys.

The brick inscribed with the architect's name is one of the oversized wood-mold variety Means preferred. As he did when he could, Means added red clay from the property to color the mortar and tie it to the place. He had the masons rake the mortar joints to create a small shadow. Jimmy Means's dedication to such details made the Holloways say, "What would Mr. Means think?"

WEST HOUSE

Means client: Dr. and Mrs. J. Herbert West.
Place: Crabapple Community, Alpharetta, Georgia.
Completion Date: June 1978.
Style: Plantation plain-style cottage (re-creation).
Contractor/builder: Larry Shirah.
The Houses of James Means, *pp. 98–99.*

Chestnut Hill is a work par excellence of James Means's special architectural art. It was the last project he completed before he died at age 75. Dr. and Mrs. J. Herbert West, Beverly and Herb, were clients and friends; a happy marriage of client and architect took place after the Wests' children were grown, when the parents needed a smaller house and wanted an adventure.

One of Means's most interesting projects, it demonstrates many reasons why his legacy is worthy of our attention. The house and the place are called Chestnut Hill because of an earlier house in Virginia by that name belonging to several generations of Dr. West's family. The house stands on a hillside at the end of a sharply curving driveway that Means laid out as part of the twenty-three-acre compound in the Crabapple community of north Fulton County, Georgia. The Wests moved into Chestnut Hill in June 1978; Means died nine months later, before he could finish another project.

Means had long admired a small story-and-a-half, elegantly simple, vernacular house built in 1820 at Bon Aire, which is in Houston County, south of Macon, in the part of middle Georgia from which Means came. He had studied, sketched, and measured the aban-

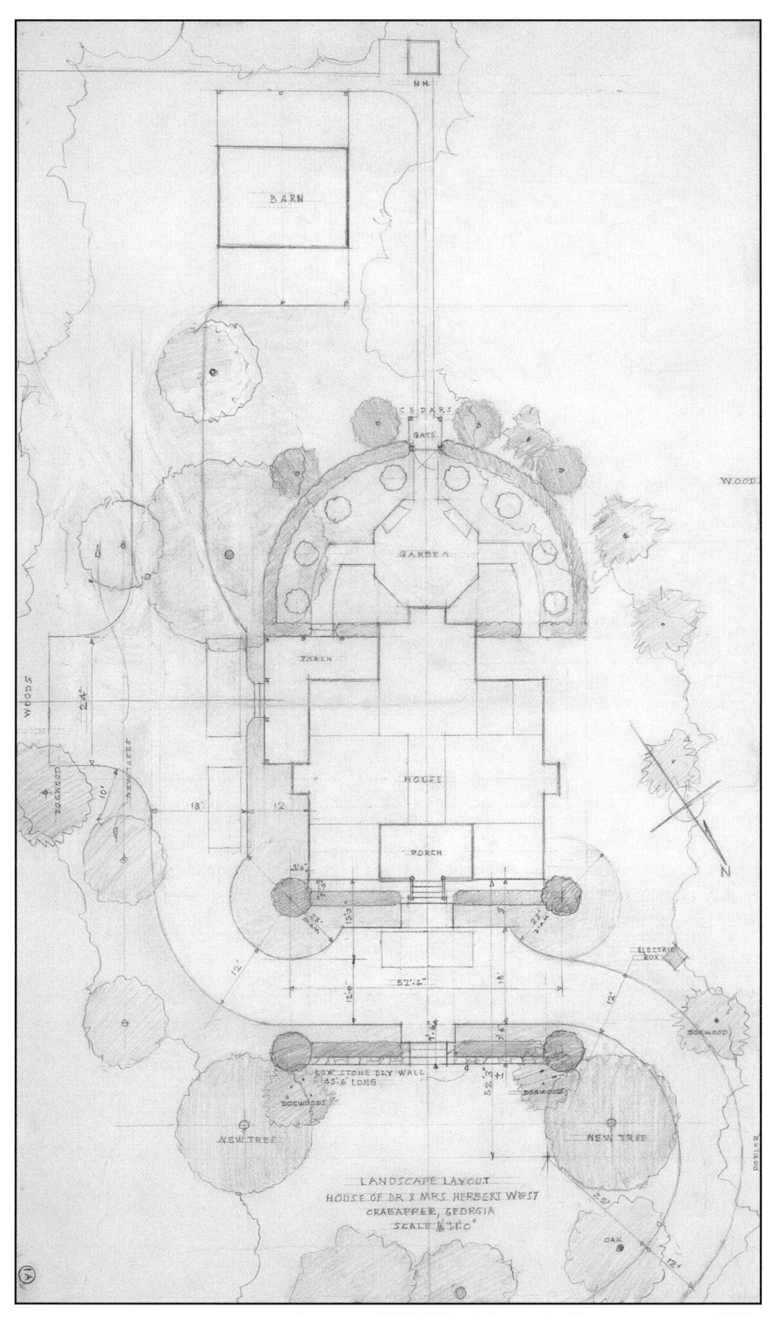

Opposite: Entrance elevation. Left: Means's landscape layout. Above: View of east side of house.Below left: Barn.

doned house with the idea of someday duplicating it, or at least incorporating some of its handsome lines into one of his own designs, as he did with other precedents he especially admired. The logic of its symmetrical entrance façade and central hall plan, the entrance porch loggia with three doorways, and the cant of its roof appealed to him. Finally he drew a plan with the old house as the basis of the concept. In the Wests he found the people to help him carry out his quest. Together, they re-created Means's Bon Aire dream house, for it was too far gone to be salvaged. They made a rural Georgia–style jewel box entirely of old recycled materials, but none of them came from the Bon Aire model.

Because even the parts of the Bon Aire farmhouse could not be saved, the Wests and their architect began a long search to find usable old materials to recycle. Together they traveled many Georgia backroads. The Wests say that Means "traveled light, with only a toothbrush." Dr. West took time off from his medical practice to haul much of the old lumber, window panes, and other treasures, such as old doors, hinges, and bricks.

According to the Wests, James Means is "Saint Jimmy." He helped them to save part of Georgia's farm heritage on their own Chestnut Hill. They now have nineteen buildings in all, a private museum of rural Georgia culture that James Means loved and knew so much about. Among others are a log cabin guest house, a split-log corn crib, a smokehouse, a privy, and a small 1813 doctor's office from the Alpharetta area. The Means-designed barn was built from old cypress and has often stored old building materials.

Hobby is hardly the word for their labor intensive lovefest of hard work. Their builder, Larry Shirah, was the hero who helped bring the plans and dreams into three-dimensional reality. The Wests' 2,800-square-foot cottage was, shall we say, Saint Jimmy's last earthly/heavenly mansion, the true home of the Georgia classicist's heart. The actual residents, of course, are his happy clients, still loving it these many years later, as Metropolitan Atlanta slowly but surely encroaches on their formerly rural Shangri-la.

West House.
Above: Entrance hall.
Opposite: Top: Living room. Bottom: Floor plan.

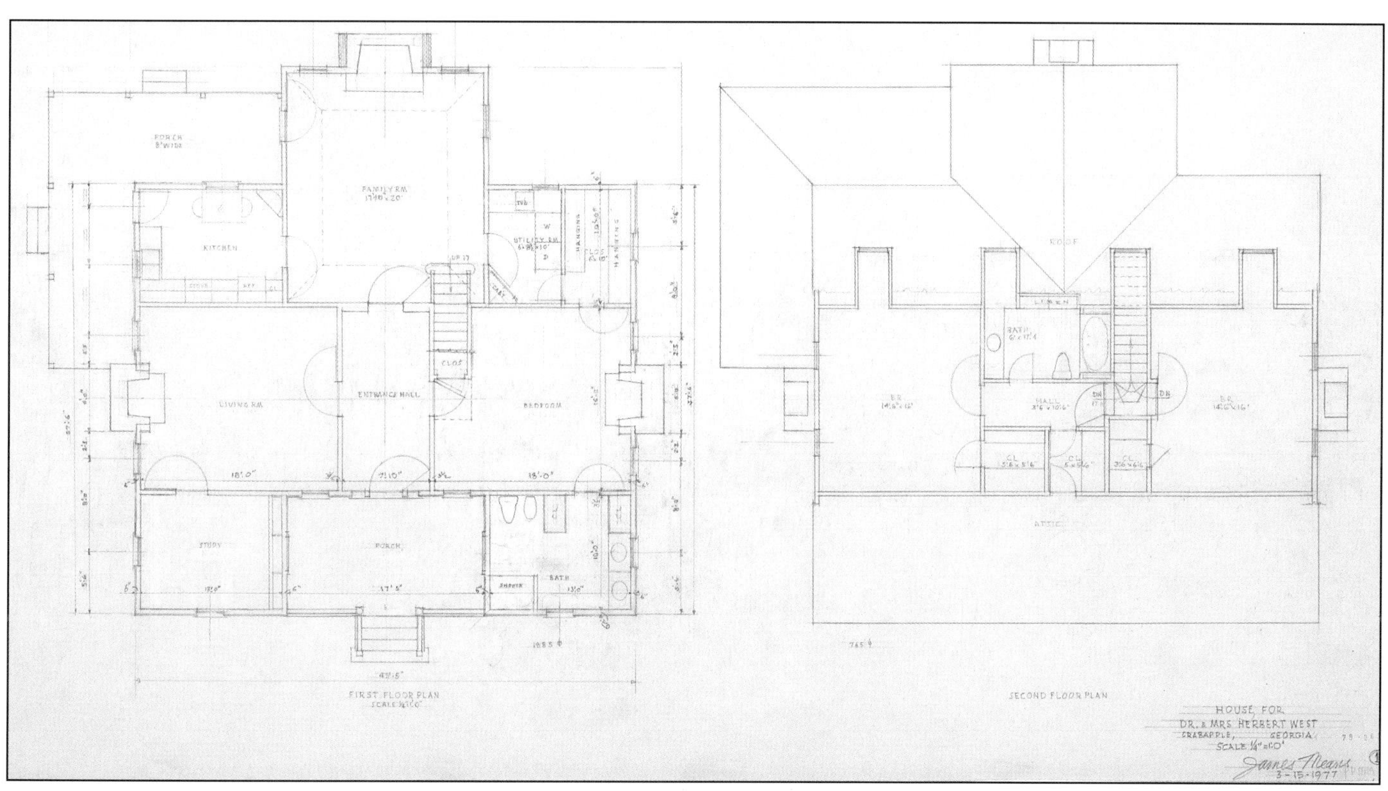
FAMILY RM.
KITCHEN
LIVING RM.
ENTRANCE HALL
BEDROOM
STUDY
PORCH
BATH
ROOF
ATTIC
FIRST FLOOR PLAN
SECOND FLOOR PLAN
HOUSE FOR
DR. & MRS. HERBERT WEST
CRABAPPLE, GEORGIA
SCALE 1/4" = 1'0"
James Means
3-15-1977

Conclusion

James Collier (Jimmy) Means died February 8, 1979, from injuries suffered in a car accident on a Saturday night in early January. He never regained consciousness; he was seventy-five. In 1978 he had completed his last long-term project, which concludes Selected Works. For Dr. and Mrs. J. Herbert West, it is a farmhouse replication of old materials on over twenty landscaped acres in northwest Fulton County, Georgia. The Wests have an expression, "According to Saint Jimmy."

At the time Means died, he was in the middle of building in Atlanta's Buckhead for Mr. and Mrs. Kenneth A. Anderberg a house that follows in this conclusion as completed by Mr. and Mrs. Louis Huff. Just off of West Wesley Road, near the Tench Coxe house (page 134), it is also in the mansard roof French provincial mode of the Coxe house and the nearby Montgomery house of 1954–56, Means's first house project on his own. He would have approved of the absolute symmetry and balance of this life-and-death coincidence. The Huffs' splendid completion of the Anderbergs' project is a fitting tribute to both the late Jimmy Means and the late Jeannie Keller Huff, who died in 1999 just as the Huffs were beginning the end of their loving home creation.

On the evening in January 1979 when his car was smashed by a careless driver, Means was driving to pick up architect and close (nearly lifelong) friend Philip Shutze (1890–1982) for a Saturday Night Club session at the home of Shutze's cousin, Catherine Maynard, on Glen Arden Drive in Buckhead, just off West Paces Ferry Road. She was the daughter of Shutze's aunt, Catherine Erwin. Means and Shutze had placed her house there, moving and renovating it, when it had to be relocated because of the construction of I-75. (No wonder Means and his clients loved the pre-expressway past!)

Had the two associates arrived, they would have been near Dr. Waldo Moore's Means house (page 118) in the new enclave of houses built on the old James Dickey property. (Dr. Moore was one of Means's doctors; another was Dr. Herbert West; both were clients and friends, a typical pattern in Means's life.) When Means started work as an office boy for Hentz, Reid & Adler in 1917, the Dickey house was being built. By the time it was completed, Means was drafting and assisting the office in various ways other than errands. That was the first big Reid-designed house in the Buckhead suburbs, when the area was just beginning to be developed. That Philip Shutze had done some of the drafting for the Dickey house again brings things full circle with the geometric clarity that Means and Shutze admired.

Philip Shutze had played an unusually important role in Means's life and career; it is fitting that he was involved in the final tragic drama. Shutze had been in Means's wedding to Mary Mangham in 1941, and, according to Jimmy's best man, architect Linton H. Young, Shutze was even included on the Meanses' wedding trip to Virginia to visit historic houses. When Shutze died in October 1982 he left Mary Means $10,000 in his will. We can only speculate that Shutze regretted that Means and Mary had later divorced, but Mary Mangham Means reports that the night her former husband's car was hit head-on, he was still wearing his wedding ring, and he had never really considered himself anything but legally divorced from the mother of Mary, Jimmy Jr., and Sally.

Means's work had largely been his life since he had become Neel Reid's drafting hands. In many ways a private, unassuming, and unpretentious person, not seeking the spotlight, he sought faithfully to serve the art of architecture, working daily to realize the classicist ideal of timeless, enduring design. Basing his designs in the most beautiful historical precedents, he favored the eighteenth and nineteenth centuries in America, especially the Southern region, and old Europe. His honeymoon even became a Cook's tour of historic Virginia, with a colleague along for good measure.

He was the ultimate protégé of the Georgia school of classicists, an exemplar, as was Edward Vason Jones, his only partner. Shutze never made him a partner. Toward the end of

Philip Shutze's career in the 1940s and early '50s, it is this writer's opinion that there should have been a firm called Shutze & Means, as there would be Jones & Means, but that was not to be.

In 1977, when the Classical America society of New York City recognized Philip Shutze as "the greatest living classical architect," they might have paid some notice to his longtime associate James Means. Jimmy Means was no doubt proud of his colleague and friend in the Georgia school, with whom he had worked since 1917. Later, Edward Jones would also be recognized with the Arthur Ross Award of that society (1983), "for continued excellence and integrity in the application of classical ideals."

James Means was not nationally known in this lifetime, but he was certainly in the same league with other classicist architects who practiced in the South, including Shutze and Jones. Among those were William L. Bottomley (1883–1951), the Georgian revivalist of Richmond and New York, a generation older than Means; Richard Koch (1889–1971), of New Orleans, Louisiana, who synthesized regional idioms; John Staub (1892–1981), of Houston, Texas; and A. Hays Town (1903–), of Baton Rouge, Louisiana. O'Neil Ford, of San Antonio, Texas, who was born in 1905 and died in 1982, was Means's only exact contemporary. All of them have been well recognized for their domestic architecture, which has been one of the premier cultural expressions of the South.

Like Means in Georgia, O'Neil Ford was interested in early buildings of his state, indigenous materials, and the integration of crafts and design. Unlike Means, however, Ford became involved with the academic world, as a visiting professor at Harvard and the University of Texas, and received many honors, including the Thomas Jefferson Award from the University of Virginia in 1967.

Anderberg-Huff House. Entrance elevation.

On the other hand, James Means was the sole subject of a book, *The Houses of James Means*, in the year of his death, a project initiated by his client-friends even before his accidental death and a high honor and accolade, indeed.

Now, twenty-two years later, *The Architecture of James Means* is published by the newly formed Southern Architecture Foundation, Inc., as its inaugural project. Although *Classical America IV*, a periodical of Classical America, honored Philip Shutze in 1977, a hardbound, full-fledged book about Shutze did not come until 1989. In it James Means is given only a supporting role, as though he had not been a vital part of Shutze's practice, when they were in fact, in the 1940s and early 1950s, a team, as he and Edward Jones had been during the same period.

Perhaps the true test of a legacy is followers who clearly acknowledge their debt with work that respects the mastery of a mentor. (Means always acknowledged the importance first of Neel Reid and then of Philip Shutze, in his training, approach, and career.) Means himself had been the outcome of a "school" instead of a college, a follower who generously became the leader in developing the architectural culture of his clients and, by example, the region.

He had younger architects, furthermore, budding classicists, who admired him tremendously. One of the best of these has been Norman Davenport Askins, a native of the beautiful Mountain Brook suburb of Birmingham, Alabama, a 1966 graduate of the Georgia Tech architectural program, with an additional degree in 1968 from the University of Virginia's prestigious master's program in architectural history. Askins became aware of what he called " James Means's distinctive architectural practice" when he was a student at Georgia Tech. The first Means house he saw was the home of Dr. and Mrs. John O. Ellis (page 76) having been taken there by a fellow student, a cousin of John Ellis. He instantly became a "Means fan," he says. "This was a person I wanted to work for and learn from. I quickly discovered that the office was in a garage apartment on East Paces Ferry behind an antique store, and I was off to meet the talented Mr. Means and apply for a summer drafting job. Dressed in khakis and a flannel shirt, he opened the door to his office, which was as modest as he. My only success was a brief, but interesting conversation."

That was in 1965. Askins continued: "Thirteen years later (1978) when I returned to Atlanta to start my practice, Dr. Waldo Moore invited me to have lunch with Mr. Means and him to discuss traditional residential architecture. I will never forget Mr. Means's generosity in offering me his support and advice on my new endeavor. At his suggestion, I phoned him a few times when I needed to know sources for specialty materials, the best contractors and millworkers, materials, etc., but I never saw him again."

Perhaps Askins's most telling testimony for this book follows: "Our brief friendship did not end with his death, however. It has been [over] the past twenty years that I have really gotten to know Mr. Means: I have worked on no less than ten of his houses, studied his drawings and details, and have heard many insightful stories about him as told by his adoring clients."

Both the Means houses chosen to conclude this book have felt architect Norman Askins's subtle understanding of the spirit and detail of James Means's architecture. The first was unfinished at the time of Means's death in 1979. The Kenneth and Beverly Anderberg house was purchased incomplete in June 1980 by Louis and Jeannie Huff; the steep driveway was unpaved and muddy. By 1985 the exterior was largely the way they wanted it, with the help of Norman Askins. Together with the late Jeannie Huff (who died in 1999), of Jean Keller Huff Designs, and Louis Huff, Askins expanded the master suite with a dressing and bathroom addition, with garages below, new front steps and stoop and a walk with garden wall and gate. Norman also designed a massive living room mantel, which seems like part of the French provincial character of Means's original conception. Last, Askins redesigned the existing library paneling.

Having no Means drawings from which to work, Norman

Anderberg-Huff House.
Left: Stair hall with view into living room.
Above: Garden path and gate.

measured the house, and he and the Huffs together completed this Means house. The house and garden as photographed in May 2000 reflect Means, Askins, the Huffs, and other advisors on whom the owners have called to complete the proverbial picture of perfection that Means would undoubtedly be pleased has occurred. (It is said that Means never built a home for himself because he could "never please myself.")

The Anderberg-Huff house is a tribute to both the difficult-to-please Jimmy Means and Jeannie Huff, also a perfectionist. In honoring his late wife, as he continues to do in this splendid home, Louis Huff is to be congratulated on continuing the Means tradition into the twenty-first century.

The other concluding house is that of Mrs. Nancy MacDougald in the West Paces Ferry section of the northwest Atlanta suburbs. Completed in 1964, it is described in *The Houses of James Means* as "a grey shingled New England farmhouse that seems to be in the country, although it is two blocks from an expressway." In 1991 Mrs. MacDougald's house became the property of James and Nancy Braithwaite. Mrs. Braithwaite, as was the late Jeannie Huff, is a well-known interior designer. When in November 2000 *House Beautiful* published this house and garden and her interior decoration; she was quoted, "I believe in simplicity."

In 1998 the Braithwaites commissioned Norman Askins to make alterations and additions in keeping with the Means and MacDougald original. They added a new family room wing, kitchen, and stone-clad master bathroom-dressing room wing. They remodeled the existing master bath and closet and added a new stone garage and pergola connector, a new wooden bridge with a new property entrance, and a new stone "spring house" outbuilding. All in all, it is an elegant simplicity worthy of James Means.

Nancy Braithwaite says her rule in altering the house has been, "What would Jimmy do?" What could be simpler than that? And how apt as a pledge to the posthumous influence of James Collier Means, whose vision for each of his creations he found almost impossible to compromise when the style had been set. Each house was an essay composed for the individual client within the realm of what he thought suitable. Sometimes he and the client "fell out," sometimes permanently, and he never went back, but they usually agreed to disagree—and Jimmy Means prevailed.

That is what "Jimmy would do," because his work was persistently his life since he became Neel Reid's hands. What higher accolade could be expressed for a Georgia classicist, since Neel Reid was the godfather of that distinguished architectural coterie?

Jimmy Means had refined the classicist tradition and carried it to sincere, precise, authentic, artistic expressions. The mainstream of architecture and life, however, was not flowing in serenely classic directions, but racing stressfully at breakneck speed along the frantic expressways of modern megalopolis America, the South included. That Jimmy Means was doomed at age seventy-five by an out-of-control automobile driver is certainly a sad irony. (His car, always the most modest model, had propelled him down many a country road in search of history.) Yet a beautiful, cherished legacy survives, a new heritage of homes, as this book testifies on every page. As with Christopher Wren, if you seek his monument, look around.

MacDougald-Braithwaite House.
Above: Front elevation. Below left: Rear elevation. Below right: Living room.

Appendix I: Introduction to The Houses of James Means (1979), *by Mary Catherine Means*

This essay, written by Jimmy Means's daughter, Mary Catherine, for the first book on her father's work, The Houses of James Means, *is reproduced as printed in 1979.*

Atlanta's residential architecture has long been distinguished by its strong roots in the past. The influence of traditional styles is ever present, from the classical grandeur of the West Paces Ferry mansions down through the countless suburban colonial houses and apartment complexes which comprise the city's neighborhoods.

It is difficult, if not impossible, to tell which came first, the taste or the tastemakers. But it is unquestionable that much of the look of Atlanta is due to the work of a handful of architects and designers, among whom Neel Reid and Philip T. Shutze most easily come to mind.

In this tradition James Means continued to produce uniquely elegant classical houses until quite recently, yet he was relatively unknown beyond his circle of clients and staunch admirers. As more scholarly attention is paid to the undercurrent of classicism in twentieth century architecture, James Means may achieve recognition unafforded him during his lifetime.

Mr. Means was born in 1904, the son of Jessie Embree Means and John Francis Means, a general building contractor and inventor from Macon who moved his family and business to Atlanta's West End in 1906. In daily contact with his father's construction activities, Jimmy developed an interest in building at an early age.

In 1917 he became an office boy in the architectural firm of Hentz, Reid, and Adler. Even though he only worked part-time, he very quickly became fascinated by the process of design and was eager to learn more. Neel Reid was taken with the inquisitive young man and generously began to teach him the elements of architecture. This tutelage and apprenticeship was to last nine years, interrupted finally by Reid's untimely death.

Upon graduation from Tech High in 1921 and at the urging of Reid and others in the office, Means enrolled in Georgia Tech to study architecture formally, but soon decided that while sitting in class he was actually missing the chance for a better architectural education back in the office. He returned to Reid's side. In 1923 Philip Trammell Shutze, who had won the Prix de Rome in 1915, joined the firm, replacing Neel Reid upon his death in 1926. The two older architects exerted very strong influence on Means' design consciousness and visual vocabulary.

James Means was possibly the last living architect trained in the 18th century manner, before the schooling of architects became institutionalized and codified. The office library contained many rare 18th and 19th century treatises on architecture which became the basis for Means' education. He learned as Christopher Wren's generation did—from apprenticeship to master designers and from the original books. Consequently, his sense of classical proportion was exact and profound. All designs by James Means were purely Means, but several have fooled experts who guessed them to be genuine 18th century buildings

Although the firm's name changed over the years to reflect newer partnership arrangements, Means remained with Philip Shutze until the firm was dissolved in 1950, only interrupting his tenure with a brief stint at the Department of Treasury during the Depression and by war years spent at Fort MacPherson. His skills grew and matured as he worked for Shutze on such office commissions as the Fulton County Medical Society Building, Emory University Hospital, Glenn Memorial Church and numerous residences.

In 1950 the office closed and Means moved to Albany, Georgia, to work in partnership with Edward Vason Jones for three years. Among his clients, during this period, were Angus Alberson in Albany and Ola Aultman in Warwick.

Means had married the former Mary Mangham in 1941 and had a growing family of two daughters, Sally and Mary Catherine, and a son, James, Jr., who was fatally stricken with childhood cancer while in Albany. Means ended the partnership and moved his family back to Atlanta in 1954 to obtain proper treatment for the boy, who died two years later.

Means' first commission on his own in Atlanta was a large French house for Mr. and Mrs. Arthur L. Montgomery. Others found in this book followed. He always worked alone, without a draftsman or secretary. Remarkably, from 1950 until his death in 1979, he was responsible for forty-nine houses and nine major remodelings. Another sixteen houses were designed but not built. In addition, he was the architect for the State of Georgia for the reconstruction of Stone Mountain Plantation, finding, moving and reassembling seventeen buildings from various locations around the state, to create an example of an early working Georgia plantation.

James Means' work can be roughly divided into three main categories: American, Continental and restorations or reconstructions. The American buildings are distinguished by their elegant symmetry and accurate proportions. Interiors are formal, often featuring paneled rooms, generous hallways and graceful staircases. Accurate to the smallest detail, the houses are nevertheless comfortable and imminently livable by contemporary standards.

Residences in the French style are also characterized by their formal dignity, uncanny proportion and careful detailing. As is the case with all houses by Means, virtually every element, even down to window mullions, was custom designed and fabricated.

The moved, reassembled or restored houses present a wide variety of interesting Southern forms. Each brought different challenges to individual problems of moving and reconstruction.

Means was noted for his desire to use old building materials whenever possible, especially for flooring and paneling. Not only did he consider them to be superior in quality to contemporary versions, but some earlier materials, such as heart pine, were no longer available. Over the years he had become well-known to building salvage dealers in several states and, in addition, possessed an almost instinctive ability to spot an abandoned early 19th century farmhouse in an overgrown field or behind a distant hill. Impossible to preserve *in situ*, these buildings provided flooring, paneling and other items for newer houses. Means tried to involve the client in the search whenever possible. Owners of Means houses still have anecdotes of backroads odysseys, spiced with encounters with livestock and suspicious farmers.

Means' recycling approach came to its logical conclusion in one of his last completed commissions, the residence of Dr. and Mrs. J. Herbert West in Crabapple, which is almost entirely built from antique materials, including the window glass.

James Means was never noted as a businessman. His cost estimates were almost always far from accurate. He expected his clients to understand and accept his perfectionism and had little patience with the inevitable cost over-runs. Fortunately, most James Means clients knew that building one of his houses was never estimated with fiscal accuracy.

One cannot deny the quality of craftsmanship that is Means' hallmark, however. Few were the masons, carpenters and contractors who could produce the intricate details and quality his designs required. He had a tendency to use the same contractors with whom he had already worked whenever possible. Elaborate paneling, custom windows and doors presented millwork challenges which were often met in the early years by Jesse Jones of Cornelia and later almost exclusively by Jim Girdler of W. P. Stephens Lumber Company, Marietta.

As a person, Jimmy Means enjoyed a rare relationship with the owners of his houses, due in part to the long personal involvement he had in each design. He was a man of remarkably simple tastes and had little interest in personal recognition or material status. Divorced for many years, he lived alone in a modest house in Alpharetta, gardening with a passion and continuing to design houses until his death in an automobile accident in February, 1979.

Although he practiced architecture for over fifty years, it is ironic that James Means never was a registered architect, for without formal training he was unable to pass the structural engineering elements in the state examination. Yet his mark has been indelibly stamped on Atlanta and many other southern communities and on the lives of his many friends and clients.

Mary Catherine Means

Appendix II: *James Collier Means and the Georgia School of Classicists*

A school: persons who hold a common doctrine or follow the same teacher. A group of artists under a common influence.

To school: to teach or drill in a specific knowledge or skill.

James Means (1904–79), a native of middle Georgia who grew up in Atlanta, went to school to "the Georgia school of classicists" when he began to work as an office boy in 1917 in the Atlanta firm of Hentz, Reid & Adler, the school's fountainhead.

All three of the principals of that preeminent firm had grown up in Georgia and studied architecture under the pervasive influence of the great classicist Charles McKim of McKim, Mead & White in the architecture department of Columbia University in New York City. J. Neel Reid (1885–1926) and Hal Fitzgerald Hentz (1883–1972) went into practice together in 1909 in Atlanta and Macon, Georgia. Rudolph Sartorius Adler (1889–1945) joined them in 1910 and became a partner in 1916.

The department of architecture at Georgia Institute of Technology had been founded in 1908, too late to benefit Hentz or Reid or Adler. Some of its first graduates went to work for Hentz & Reid, the firm's first corporate name. James Means graduated from Atlanta's Technical High School in 1921, all the while working for Hentz, Reid & Adler. He tried the formal architecture program at Georgia Tech for a short while but decided to work full time for the firm instead, believing that he could learn more on the job. Neel Reid was principal designer, but all three principals were excellent draftsmen and practical architects. Hentz, Reid & Adler was a sort of Atlanta beaux arts atelier or training studio, a learn-by-doing experience for all of them as the practice expanded in the years just before and after World War I.

Means also learned from some of the other architects who worked with the firm at that time. They included Ernest Daniel Ivey (1887–1966) and Lewis Edmund Crook, Jr. (1898–1967), both Georgia Tech architecture graduates, who formed Ivey & Crook in 1923; and Philip Trammell Shutze (1890–1982), another Georgia Tech and Columbia University graduate, who became the junior partner of a newly formed Hentz, Adler & Shutze in 1927, a year after Neel Reid's death.

James Means continued with Hentz, Adler & Shutze, becoming Shutze's assistant and close friend, until Shutze retired and Means formed a two-year partnership with Edward Vason Jones (1909–82) of Albany, Georgia, in 1952. At that time Means was described as having been Reid's hands.

In the 1960s and '70s Edward Jones would become a national figure, pumping new life into neoclassicism in Washington, D.C., through his work in the White House and the State Department. Largely self-taught, Jones had worked for Hentz, Adler & Shutze in the 1930s and early '40s. In 1954 the partnership of Jones & Means dissolved, and Means returned to practice alone in Atlanta, specializing in residential design. Means practiced what he had learned from his compatriots, and though he was never registered, he took classic domestic architecture to new heights on his own.

Edward Jones perhaps defined the Georgia school of classicists best when he said in a lecture at Athens, Georgia, in 1973, "Neel Reid and Philip Shutze, who followed in Reid's footsteps, were convinced that the design of a house or any structure for that matter, could not be successful unless it was correctly landscaped and properly furnished. So I religiously followed this concept." In addition, the working drawings or "plans" these classicists produced to realize their complete visions are themselves works of art, as this book demonstrates.

Some other architects who should be considered part of the Georgia school of classicists, in order of their birth, are Philip Thornton Marye (1872–1935), Atlanta; Francis Palmer Smith (1886–1971), Atlanta; James J. W. Biggers (1893–1992), Columbus; W. Elliott Dunwody, Jr. (1893–1986), Macon; Samuel Inman Cooper (1894–1974), Atlanta; Henry J. Toombs (1896–1967), Atlanta; McKendree A. (Mack) Tucker (1896–1972), Atlanta; C. Wilmer Heery (1904–89), Athens; Albert Howell (1904–74), Atlanta; Clement J. Ford (1906–92), Atlanta; and William Frank McCall (1914–91), Moultrie.

Appendix III: Means Files at the Atlanta History Center

Mr. Means, who is associated with Edward Vason Jones here, worked for a long time with the noted architect Neel Reid. During Reid's last illness, he was not able to draw, so Mr. Means was his "hands" and would execute the drawings to his directions. Later Means did design work for Hentz, Adler & Shutze.

Louise Whiting
Albany Herald, January 27, 1952

The Atlanta History Center is the primary repository for James Means's architectural drawings. His daughter, Mary Catherine Means, donated this collection in two stages, in 1979 and in 1983. In the "Visual Arts" card file, under "Architectural Drawings A–Z: Firms and Architects" is the James Means file. It is arranged alphbetically on three-by-five-inch cards by client. (This Visual Arts file is being expanded, refined, and made ready for computerized access.)

The History Center assigned an "Mea" number to each of its files of Means drawings. The Mea numbers following are for Means's works at the History Center for clients included in this book. The drawings currently classified by the History Center as "unidentified" begin with Mea 63 and end with Mea 87. Some of these drawings have been included in the portfolio section, beginning on page 18.

Mea 1 Alberson, Mr. and Mrs. Angus A.
Mea 2 Bloom, Dr. Walter Lyon
Mea 5 Efird, Mr. and Mrs. J. Ray
Mea 6 Parker, Mr. and Mrs. William A.
Mea 7 Florence, Dr. and Mrs. Thomas J.
Mea 8 Toon, Mr. and Mrs. Ralph L., Jr.
Mea 9 Milner, Mr. and Mrs. Gene W.
Mea 10 Plowden, Mr. and Mrs. Will Best
Mea 11 Haverty, Mr. and Mrs. Rawson
Mea 12 Felker, Mr. and Mrs. George W., III
Mea 13 Martin, Mr. and Mrs. Thomas E., Jr.
Mea 15 Carr, Mr. and Mrs. Jack L.
Mea 16 Holloway, Dr. and Mrs. Alfred M.
Mea 17 Shapard, Mr. and Mrs. Robert P., III
Mea 18 Dender, Judge and Mrs. William M.
Mea 20 Bryant, Dr. and Mrs. Milton F.
Mea 21 Torrence, Mr. and Mrs. Samuel M.
Mea 22 Barrett, Mrs. H. Gould
Mea 23 Moore, Dr. and Mrs. B. Waldo
Mea 24 Browne, Dr. and Mrs. Harry Gray
Mea 25 Hennessy, Mr. and Mrs. Robert D.
Mea 26 Cavender, Mr. and Mrs. Ralph
Mea 29 MacDougal, Mr. and Mrs. Dan
Mea 30 Appleby, Mr. and Mrs. William C.
Mea 31 Ellis, Mr. and Mrs. William D.
Mea 32 Montgomery, Mr. and Mrs. Arthur L.
Mea 33 Cook, Mr. and Mrs. Marcus A., Jr.
Mea 34 Hedges, Mr. and Mrs. James R.
Mea 35 Ballard, Mr. and Mrs. McCary
Mea 36 Rooker, Mr. and Mrs. William A., Jr.
Mea 37 Coxe, Mr. and Mrs. Tench C.
Mea 38 Kennedy, Mr. and Mrs. Alfred Doby
Mea 40 Pike, Dr. and Mrs. J. Sanders
Mea 41 Bounds, Osborne, Jr.
Mea 44 West, Dr. and Mrs. J. Herbert
Mea 47 Akers, Mr. and Mrs. William B.
Mea 55 Shackelford, Frank
Mea 62 Pharr, Frank E.
Mea 105 Jones, Jesse, Sr. *
Mea 107 Kleiner, Dr. Jack*

* *These files are not yet included in the Visual Arts finding aid.*

Appendix IV: Sources

This Means monograph, as the preface details, results from a long acquaintance with the architect and admiration for his works. (The preface may be read as an adjunct to this appendix.)

My own writings about Means and his associates are sources for the present volume. In the 1980s I originated the concept "Georgia school of classicists" as a description of my understanding of Means, his mentors, and contemporaries, first in Hentz, Reid & Adler and then in Hentz, Adler & Shutze. I have written a book on Means's primary mentor, Neel Reid (1997), as well as on three of Means's Georgia contemporaries: Lewis Crook (1984), Frank McCall (1985 and 1992), and Edward Vason Jones (1995), Means's partner in the early 1950s. The latter book was especially helpful here because of the Jones archive in Albany, containing data on the Jones & Means partnership. All three of these conservative Georgia classicists remained true to traditionalism, as did Means, in the midst of a growing post–World War II modernism. (See Appendix II.)

A major source I used in the preparation of this monograph is *The Houses of James Means*, edited by the late Callie Huger Efird. Published in the fall of 1979 after Means's death earlier that year, it was a one-hundred-page tribute by some of his client-friends, when still fresh in their minds; Callie Efird and Nancy Toon were the leaders. It began as a Means house tour that had expanded, just before his accidental death, to include an illustrated book.

Mrs. Toon, who originated the Means house tour and became the book's coordinator, shared with me notes she had gathered in preparation for both the tour and the book. Some of these were facts she obtained from Means himself on many of the forty-nine houses that he and the committee had chosen to be photographed and documented.

That book was arranged by historic architectural styles; this one is arranged chronologically, a sequence that shows Means's style versatility from the beginning of his personal practice—his first house was French. This arrangement reveals the amount of work on his drawing board at one time. It provides a history of his career practicing alone.

I have three copies of *The Houses of James Means*, two of the 1975 edition and one of the 1985 reprint (slightly revised). I purchased the latter at a publication party I attended that year in the Means-designed Arthur Montgomery house, that French house referred to above. (See page 30.)

Other vitally important sources for research are his sketches and studies and the preliminary and working drawings that Mary Catherine Means, his eldest child and daughter (now of Alexandria, Virginia) donated to the Atlanta Historical Society in two stages, in 1979 and in 1983. In December 1986, Ms. Means commissioned a staff archivist there, Donald Rooney, to begin cataloguing these donated drawings. (Means assigned owner's names, not "job numbers," to his commissions, so, unlike the Hentz, Reid & Adler commissions, they cannot be indexed that way.) Rooney devised a system for the historical society (see Appendix III) which also includes the unidentified projects and drawings, some of which I have been able to identify.

My study of these drawings and some miscellaneous ones still in Ms. Means's possession, which she salvaged from her father's office after he died, have been invaluable. We have copied numerous examples of these to use throughout the book. They include floor plans, none of which were illustrated in the 1979 publication; these help to demonstrate Means's use of space and scale. These and various other sources have allowed us to enlarge the number of projects and completed commissions from the forty-nine in the 1979 tribute as well as to illustrate the beauty and interest of numerous of Means's sketches not published before.

My interviews with original, subsequent, and current owners, as photography proceeded, were of primary importance. In tracking down scores of these people, I was assisted by Mrs. Reynolds (Martha Hightower) McClatchey, who prepared a master list. James Lockhart, the principal photographer for this project, also assisted in that endeavor and, on occasion, brought written notes for me from those owners when he photographed a structure I unfortunately couldn't visit.

As always, the buildings and their sites are primary sources for understanding the architect's work. Jim Lockhart's photographs of the structures and their sites and of the drawings of them are crucial adjuncts to the text. They are an excellent stand-in for the beauty of the three-dimensional reality. Southern Architecture Foundation has published *The Architecture of James Means* as a new source for the study of the Georgia school of classicists and of one of its most outstanding members.

INTERVIEWS

I. ORIGINAL MEANS CLIENTS (and some of their relations)

Mr. and Mrs. Angus Alberson (1993, Jones & Means interview)
Eleanor Morgan (Montgomery) Atuk
Mr. Osborne Bounds (interviews 1966 –71)
Mrs. Milton F. Bryant
Mr. and Mrs. Douglas (Nancy) Bryant (son of Dr. and Mrs. Milton Bryant, and current owner of house)
Mr. and Mrs. Ralph (Harriet) Cavender
Mrs. Nancy Laird Crosswell
Judge and Mrs. William M. Dender
Mrs. J. Ray (Callie) Efird (d. 1994, 1990 interview)
Dr. and Mrs. John O. Ellis
Mr. W. Douglas Ellis, Jr. (son of, and current owner)
Mrs. George W. Felker III (original client and mother of current owner, Stephen Felker)
Dr. and Mrs. Thomas Florence
Mr. and Mrs. Rawson (Margaret) Haverty
Mrs. Robert D. Hennessy
Mrs. Alfred D. Kennedy, Sr.
Mrs. Nancy MacDougald (1989 interview)
Mr. and Mrs. Thomas E. Martin, Jr. (numerous interviews since 1981)
Mr. Arthur L. Montgomery
Mr. and Mrs. C. Talbot Nunally, Jr.
Mr. and Mrs. William A. Parker, Jr. (1989 and 1999 interviews)
Dr. and Mrs. J. Sanders Pike
Mrs. F. D. (Betty) Rayburn
Mr. William A. Rooker, Jr.
Mr. and Mrs. Robert P. (Virginia) Shapard III
Mrs. John G. Stewart
Mr. Samuel M. Torrence, Jr.
Mr. and Mrs. Ralph L. (Nancy) Toon
Dr. and Mrs. J. Herbert (Beverly) West

II. CURRENT MEANS HOUSE OWNERS

Mrs. James A. Aiken
Mrs. James C. (Nancy) Braithwaite
Mr. and Mrs. Walker Candler
Mrs. Chris (Laura) Deisley
Mrs. H. Hutson Carspecken
Mrs. Michael D. Clark
Vivian Noble DuBose
Dr. and Mrs. James B. Dunaway
Mrs. Stephen (Chris) Felker
Dr. and Mrs. Henry A. Frazier
Mr. Louis N. Huff III
Mr. and Mrs. Dexter Jordan, Jr.
Mr. and Mrs. Larry Knox
Mr. and Mrs. F. Hamilton Kuhlke
Mr. F. Bowers Parker, Jr.
Mr. and Mrs. John (Jack and Erin) Portman III
Mr. and Mrs. Jeremiah D. Luxemburger
Mrs. Craig (Ginny) Magher (1989 interview)
Mr. and Mrs. Mitchell Simmons
Mr. Wesley R. Vawter III
Mrs. Thomas M. Willingham (1989 and 1999 interview)
Mr. and Mrs. James K. Warren

III. OTHER INTERVIEWS

Mr. Norman D. Askins (architect)
Mr. David R. Byers III (interior decorator, d. 1998; interviews 1970–90s)
Mr. Edward L. Daugherty (landscape architect)
Mr. Daniel B. Franklin (landscape architect)
Mrs. James C. (Becky) Fraser (Tarrymore resident)
Mr. Kenneth Garcia, Jr. (interior decorator whose father was an associate of Means)
Mr. James (Jim) Girdler (millwork specialist)
Mrs. Gould B. (Laura Plowden) Hagler, Jr.
Mrs. Julian (Grace) Hightower (1981 interview)
Mr. William E. Huger III (parents owned the Kleiner house)
Mr. James C. Means (1970s interviews; see preface)
Mrs. Mary Mangham Means (Means's former wife; 1993 and 1999 telephone interviews)
Ms. Mary Catherine Means (Means's eldest daughter)
Mr. Donald Rooney (Atlanta Historical Society staff)
Mr. Kenneth H. Thomas, Jr. (historian and genealogist; Means family history)
Mr. Linton H. Young (lifelong friend and architect-colleague of Means, 1993 interview)

Selected Bibliography

PUBLISHED MATERIALS: BOOKS

Baldwin, William P., Jr. *Plantations of the Low Country, South Carolina, 1697–1865*. Greensboro, North Carolina: Legacy Publications, 1985.

Bloomfield, Sir Reginald. *A History of French Architecture, 1661–1774*. London: G. Bell and Sons, Ltd., 1921.

Bottomley, William L., ed. *Great Georgian Homes of America*. 2 vols. New York: Dover Publications, Inc., 1970.

Coffin, Lewis A., Jr., and Arthur C. Holden. *Brick Architecture of the Colonial Period in Maryland and Virginia.* New York: Architectural Book Publishing Co., 1919.

Connolly, Cyril, and Jerome Zerbe. *Les Pavillons: French Pavilions of the Eighteenth Century*. New York: The MacMillan Co., 1962.

Denmark, Ernest Ray. *Architecture of the Old South.* Atlanta, 1926. Foreword by Lewis E. Crook, Jr.

Dowell, Susan Stiles. *Great Houses of Maryland*. Centerville, Maryland: Tidewater Publishers, 1988.

Dowling, Elizabeth Meredith. *American Classicist: The Architecture of Philip Trammell Shutze*. New York: Rizzoli International, Inc., 1989.

Efird, Mrs. J. Ray, ed. *The Houses of James Means*. Atlanta, 1979.

Foreman, H. Chandlee. *Maryland Architecture*. Cambridge, Maryland: Tidewater Publishers, 1968.

Gladney, Blanche Town. *The Architectural Style of A. Hays Town*. Baton Rouge, Louisiana: Andulaine Publication, Inc., 1985.

Griffith, Helen C., ed. *Gardens of the South*. New York: Simon and Schuster, 1985.

Haverty, Rawson. *Ain't the Roses Sweet*. Atlanta, 1989.

Hewett, Mark Alan. *The Architect & The American Country House, 1890–1940*. New Haven: Yale University Press, 1990.

Horton, Mrs. Corinne Ruth Stocker. "Savannah and Parts of the Far South," in *The Georgian Period*. Part 3, 1902.

Kimball, Fiske. *Domestic Architecture of the American Colonies and of the Early Republic*. New York: Charles Scribner's Sons, 1922.

Lane, Mills. *Architecture of the Old South: Louisiana*. New York: Abbeville Press, 1990.

Lounsbury, Carl R., ed. *An Illustrated Glossary of Early Southern Architecture and Landscape*. New York: Oxford University Press, 1994.

Mitchell, William R., Jr. *An Anniversary Collection of Seventy Homes*. Atlanta: Harry Norman, Realtors, 1999.

———. *The Garden Club of Georgia*. Atlanta: Peachtree Publishers and Garden Club of Georgia, 1989.

———. *J. Neel Reid, Architect of Hentz, Reid & Adler and the Georgia School of Classicists*. Atlanta: The Georgia Trust for Historic Preservation, 1997.

———. *Lewis Edmund Crook, Jr., Architect, 1898–1967.* Atlanta: The History Business, Inc., 1984.

Mitchell, William R., Jr., and Van Jones Martin. *Classic Atlanta.* Savannah: Golden Coast Publishing Co., 1991.

———. *Landmark Homes of Georgia, 1733–1983.* Savannah: Golden Coast Publishing Co., 1982.

Morgan, Keith N., and Charles A. Platt: *The Artist as Architect.* New York: Architectural History Foundation, 1985.

Newsome, Lisa B., ed. *Historic Houses of the South.* New York: Simon & Schuster, 1984.

Newsome, Jane R., ed. *At Home in Washington-Wilkes.* Washington, Georgia: Wilkes Publishing Co., 1986.

O'Neal, William B., and Christopher Weeks. *William Lawrence Bottomley in Richmond.* Charlottesville: University Press of Virginia, 1985.

Nichols, Frederick Doveton, and Frances Benjamin Johnston. *The Early Architecture of Georgia.* Chapel Hill: University of North Carolina Press, 1957.

Perkerson, Medora Field. *White Columns in Georgia.* New York: Rhinehart and Co., Inc., 1982.

Raphael, Morris. *Weeks Hall, the Master of the Shadows.* Detroit: Harlo Press, 1981.

Simmons, Frances Hames, and Barbara R. Thompson. *Faith and Fabric.* Decatur, Georgia: Pathway Communications Group, 1994.

Smith, J. Frazer. *White Pillars.* New York: Wm. Hellman, Inc., 1951.

Vetter, Cyril E. *The Louisiana Houses of A. Hays Town.* Baton Rouge: Louisiana State University Press, 1999.

Ware, William Rotch, ed. *The Georgian Period: Measured Drawings of Colonial Work.* New York: American Architect.

Waterman, Thomas Tileston. *The Mansions of Virginia, 1706–1776.* Chapel Hill: University of North Carolina Press, 1945.

Whitehead, Russell F., ed. *The White Pine Series of Architectural Monographs.* Boston, 1915–36.

Whiffen, Marcus. *The Eighteenth-Century Houses of Williamsburg.* Williamsburg, Virginia: The Colonial Williamsburg Foundation, 1960.

Periodicals

Beswick, Paul G. "An Enchanting Garden Retreat." *Southern Accents* 4 (Spring 1981): 50–53.

Booth, Michael. "Rebuilding an Antebellum Country Place." *Southern Homes* 9 (September 1991): 52–55.

Bryant, H. Stafford Jr. "Two Domestic Architects in the South: Neel Reid and William L. Bottomley." *Classical America* 1 (1972): 30–36.

Burrell, Diane D. "A Loving Restoration, The Hill-Pike House in Cobb County, Georgia." *Southern Accents* 7 (January-February 1984): 76–85.

Cash, Sarah. "The Homespun House." *The Atlanta Journal and Constitution* (Sunday, 27 May 1979): H2, H6.

Foster, William Dewey, ed. "French Architecture." *The Tuileires Brochures* 4. New York: Ludowici-Celadon Company, 1931–32.

Kelley, Margaret. "Le Petit Chantecaille." *Southern Accents* 3 (Winter 1980): 30–39.

Kennedy, Margaret, ed. "American Spirit, French Style." *House Beautiful* 128 (November 1986): 80–89.

Kleine, Erica, ed. "Pineland Estate." *Colonial Homes.* 9 (September-October 1983): 64–67, 193.

Masten, Susannah. "Built to Endure." *Southern Accents* 7 (November-December 1984): 126–32, 142, 146.

Mitchell, William R., Jr. "The Architecture of James Means, Georgia Classicist." *Southern Homes* 7 (March/April 1989): 84–97.

Pittel, Christine. "High Contrast, Atlanta Designer Nancy Braithwaite. . . ." *House Beautiful* 142 (November 2000): 174–83.

"Portfolio of Current Architecture, Hentz, Reid & Adler." *Architectural Record* 42 (December 1917): 569–78.

Reed, Henry Hope. "America's Greatest Living Classicist Architect: Philip Trammell Shutze of Atlanta, Georgia." *Classical America* 4 (1977): 5–46.

Reiter, Ruth, ed. "Country Comfort Crafted from Pieces of the Past." *Traditional Home,* "Decorating Ideas" 1 (1980): 40–45.

Wilson, Susannah M. "A Continental Stance, In an Atlanta Palladian-Style Residence." *Southern Accents* 9 (March-April 1986): 90–95, 136.

Index of Jobs Illustrated

Index of Architects and Architectural Firms